THE PORTABLE WALTER

The Portable Walter

from the prose and poetry of Walter Lowenfels

by ROBERT GOVER

INTERNATIONAL PUBLISHERS
New York

First Edition

Library of Congress Catalog Card Number: 68-21820

Manufactured in the United States of America

Foreword

On March 4, 1954, two weeks before he was to go on trial for "subversive thoughts," Walter Lowenfels wrote his credo, in which he said, "I do not intend to disparage my profession. Rather, it's the administration that is promoting poets from the role Shelley assigned them—'unacknowledged legislators of mankind.' The administration now acknowledges poets as legislators."

Walter had not set out to become an "acknowledged legislator" of mankind, but it's the truth that he was guilty of subversive thoughts. He's still guilty of subversive thoughts and will go on being guilty of subversive thoughts as long as the human race is divided into warmaking nation-states and classes of exploiters and exploited.

Walter is a poet who feels compelled to proclaim his vision of what is possible for the human race, and his vision of that is of one people, indivisible as one people, living harmoniously, finding joy in themselves and their work and their individual differences—joy instead of bureaucratic-ordered death or a half-life in an ordered bureaucracy.

Walter's "crime" against the government of the United States is that he *believes* in integration—he believes that it's possible. Integration of each self and of the entire species. He rejects class, racial, national differences. So of course he is the enemy of the administration—any administration that administers people as properly catalogued things for profit-making. "I am humanity," he says. "I am all humanity and I want freedom, for I believe that people are essentially good."

Well, one might argue with him about whether people are, in fact, essentially good. But even the Marquis de Sade, who believed in the essential evil of humanity, was in favor of freedom. So is the John Birch Society in favor of freedom. Everybody has his own idea of what freedom is and there are those who feel some should be more free than others.

Walter's idea of freedom is a very optimistic one. He thinks, subversively enough, that if we would stop trying to control and exploit each other, if we would stop trying to inhibit the freedom of others in the name of freedom for ourselves, and if we would begin on a different basis—on the idea that we should produce what we need to live and what we want to enhance our living—on the assumption that we are beautiful and joyous and wonderful to and for each other. . . .

Walter, you see, is the poet of youth and optimism, and that's why he is portable. You can take him with you—in some secret compartment of your life where the FBI, CIA, or whatever mechanical men you happen to be up against can't reach. If no whores of the ruling class catch you carrying Walter or his ideas with you, you can take him along for the rest of your life. In fact, you can take him along forever, because he is, after all, an ageless, deathless spirit. Maybe that's why people take one look at him—his big brown eyes looking back at them guilelessly, with an innocence come by through the depths of life, of knowing evil and rejecting it—why people take one look at him and declare that he is "childlike."

He is—like Methuselah. He is the ageless child. He is the fact that spring will come next year and he is the hope that we will keep our duly official establishment from blowing the world to atomic smithereens to "save" us—(better dead than some bright color)—he is the fact that spring will come again and again and the catastrophes of our now will become a twinkle of life eventually. Like the twinkle in his eyes as he threads his eternal optimism through the poisonous suicidal paranoia of the American here and now. That's how Walter is portable.

ROBERT GOVER

Malibu, California, 1967.

BY WALTER LOWENFELS

POETRY

Episodes & Epistles	New York	1925
Finale of Seem	London	1929
Apollinaire	Paris	1930
Elegy for D. H. Lawrence	Paris	1932
The Suicide	Paris	1932
Sonnets of Love and Liberty	New York	1955
American Voices	New York	1959
Song of Peace	New York	1959
Some Deaths	Highlands, N.C.	1964
Land of Roseberries	Mexico City	1965
Translations from Scorpius	Monmouth, Me.	1966
Love Letters: Later Collected Poems	in preparation	

PAMPHLET POEMS

Steel 1937	1937
American Voices	1953
The Prisoners	1954

PLAY

U.S.A. With Music	Paris	1930

ANTHOLOGIES

Walt Whitman's Civil War	New York	1960
Selections from Leaves of Grass	New York	1961
Poets of Today: A New American Anthology	New York	1964
Where is Vietnam? American Poets Respond	New York	1967
New Jazz Poets	New York	1967

Prose

To an Imaginary Daughter	New York	1964
The Poetry of My Politics	Homestead, Fla.	1968
My Many Lives	in preparation	
Loving You in the Fallout	in preparation	
The Life of Fraenkel's Death (with Howard McCord)	in preparation	

NOVELS BY ROBERT GOVER

A Trilogy:

One-Hundred Dollar Misunderstanding	New York	1962
Here Goes Kitten	New York	1964
J. C. Saves	in production	
The Maniac Responsible	New York	1963
Poorboy At The Party	New York	1966

Contents

THE PORTABLE WALTER

1

My Many Lives

EDITOR'S INTRODUCTION

In the America of our day, the word Communism is hardly a word at all—it's more like a war whoop or an electric shock treatment than a word you can look up in a dictionary and find the meaning of. Our nation is thick with rumors that life in a country that calls itself Communist is almost as bad as being poor and black in Mississippi. The sound of the word has become so emotionally hot that to utter it as other than a foul curse is, in some circles, tantamount to treason. And to lift it from the context of propaganda and examine it with cool curiosity is practically unthinkable. Therefore, I feel it is well to begin this collection of Walter's writings with Part II of his autobiography, MY MANY LIVES, in which he recalls his days as a Communist activist and tells us what he was thinking and feeling at the time, and what was happening to him.

The omitted Part I is about 200 typewritten pages, unpub-

lished at this time. It's about how Walter left his family's thriving butter business and went to Europe to develop as a poet. He tells of the literary scene of the Paris he knew, of Henry Miller, T. S. Eliot, Ford Madox Ford, Richard Aldington, Sam Putnam and Ezra Pound; he tells of marrying Lillian and becoming a father, of splitting a poetry prize with e. e. cummings, and of his growing concern over the rise of fascism in Germany and Italy.

Part II begins with Walter's return to the States, back to selling butter from 9 AM *to 5* PM, *writing poetry in his "non-butter time." It recaps why and how he got into Communist activities, joining the staff of the* Daily Worker's *Pennsylvania edition, and of some events he covered for that newspaper.*

It's done in Walter's collage *style, like pasting up mementos on a wall and inspecting them—letters to friends, tales and poems, held together with bits of straight narrative. It's a man remembering a time in his life when he left poetry for politics, developed a political prose-poetry style and, finally, returned refreshed and renewed to poetry, and to a style that is all his and is uniquely suited to saying what he has to say. I think it will interest contemporary peace and civil rights activists to follow Walter's career back in the '30s—picketing the White House and mounting other "agitations." Above all, I think that to have Walter, the American Communist, tell about himself his own way will interest those of my countrymen who have never been directly exposed to an American Communist.*

R. G.

My Many Lives

From November 1935 to February 1937, I made the big switch in reverse: this time from poetry back to the butter business. Some critics have written that after my Paris poems the Communist Party performed a lobotomy on me and that was why I gave up poetry. The fact is much simpler.

After I had finished *The Suicide* in Paris (the third elegy in my series *Some Deaths*), I felt I had nothing more to say. The thread of what I was trying to do in that long poem got so tenuous at times that I used to pin up my thesis on the wall in front of the desk at 9 rue Val de Grace: "Humanity is killing itself and doesn't even know it."

So, the winter of 1934-35 found us in New York. Our Paris days had ended–geographically. The letters written in that period–from New York, Brooklyn, and Union City, and New City, N. Y. to Henry Miller and Michael Fraenkel in Paris–show what I was going through trying to make the switch. One of them follows.

To Michael Fraenkel and Henry Miller, December 11, 1935:

Before I continue, bear in mind I am now successfully leading two lives. (Note: the important thing is to be able efficiently to organize your schizoid condition.) I butter from nine to five and then I change into a butterfly and go ahead with poems. There was a moment there a few weeks ago, on my return from Iowa, when I was fluttering a bit: bought and sold a car of butter and wiped out the profit before I settled into the new schizoid rhythm, but that is over and I am finally reopening in a permanently bullish position.

It is a marvelous thing to get all your ideas operating between 5 PM and 9 AM, rather than vice versa. Not to get one single thought after the bell strikes nine: that is the final victory over Time. I call my non-butter time "Paris time."

Yes, one hand for butter, one eye for poems. The simultaneous operator—always two phones at the ear, one for the butter exchange, the other to Fraenkel or Miller. This is the new battlefront where you get so shot full of holes that instead of being separate little pieces you are all holes. The New Man—his spirit is ventilated—the Schizoid Triumph.

Simultaneously, Lillian is barricading the Brazilian Consulate, shouting at the Assistant Secretary to the Assistant Vice Consul: "Down with Brazilian nuts; up with the Coffee Revolution!" The two blue-coated cops at the door take off their hats at the sight of Mother Lil speaking revolutionary Spanish. Everybody immediately lies down and takes a siesta in Battery Park.

All this leaves out the children. My boy, I assure you, after a survey of Brooklyn, it is a world of baby carriages. The future in action—sweeping, tier after tier, over us.

Yes, that is where you will go down—all of you. From Lapland, from Tierra del Fuego, from Flatbush, from Baffins Bay—the baby carriages, wheeling, struggling pushing, sweeping all before them to the Black Sea at Odessa.

We will speak of this among the oysters, my pearl.

Gurgle,
Mollusk.

My Paris days really ended in the United States with the publication of *Steel 1937*. In this collection of poems about the Spanish Civil War and the CIO drive to organize Little Steel, I tried to carry on the technical discoveries I had made in Paris, and to apply them to the new social viewpoint that I had acquired, largely from books.

With the foreword to *Steel 1937*—an open letter to Philip Murray, who led the 1937 steel organizing drive of the CIO—I began to move forward to a different relation with a different audience from that symbolized by Fraenkel and Miller.

January 31, 1938

Open letter to Philip Murray,
Steelworkers Organizing Committee, Pittsburgh, Pa.

Beginning with the Memorial Day Massacre in South Chicago, 18 workers were killed in the spring and early summer of 1937. These deaths can be traced to the U.S. Steel side in the offensive against the people and their right to organize. While it was a coincidence that the bombardment of the people of Almería, Spain, by the fascists, took place without warning on the same day as the Chicago Massacre, the internal and external factors involved are, to my mind, the same.

In our day, attacks on the people anywhere are attacks on the people everywhere. Thus, the struggle people are making thousands of miles off, in China, or here at home seem to many to be for the same thing, the right to live in a democratic way. In the long run this becomes a struggle against the shells made of steel.

The immediate reference of the title, *Steel 1937*, is, however the Little Steel strike, 1937. While I have not asked their permission, nor yours, it seems natural to address this book through you to the hundreds of thousands of steel workers and their families who were most immediately involved. In this struggle they represented the vanguard of all democratic people. The rights they struggled to obtain for themselves are rights the people as a whole share with them. The lives lost in their struggle are a public heritage and a public responsibility which we also share.

It is true that the people win many victories without an immediate loss of lives, and we have songs and will have more to celebrate them. But the peaceful victories have behind them a long history—Homestead . . . the Steel Strike of 1919. Each victory of the people arises over lives they had to sacrifice to steel, even though such lives may have been lost elsewhere, or at some other time.

Rosa Luxemburg's life was one of them. Her place in a book called *Steel* will be clear to those who know that the setback the people's cause suffered in Germany, 1919, was due to its betrayal by misleaders among them. There is an internal as well as an external struggle that goes on. Both represent death forces which are included in this book in the word "steel." Out of such death forces, and the ability to overcome them, the life of the people takes organizational shape, and the dreams of individual and social life, including poems, goes on.

After *Steel 1937*, I gave up verse entirely for 16 years. The inadequacy of the book had convinced me that I couldn't make the switch as a writer until I made the switch as a person. We moved to Philadelphia, and I began, as a rank-and-filer, to become active in the working-class and civil-rights movements.

Jukebox in the Coalfields

Between 1939 and 1955, for 16 years, I worked first as reporter, later as editor, on the Pennsylvania edition of the *Daily Worker*. I was already in my 40's; I had no easy fluency with words; I knew what I wanted to say, but it was hard for me to say it rapidly. I had to learn how to sit at a typewriter and pound it out. I wrote thousands of words during those years—most of them about Negro workers, about coal miners and steel workers. I learned to talk with them, to listen to them, to be guided by them.

During one coal strike I flew from Philadelphia to Pittsburgh. J., the Communist organizer in Washington County, met me at the airport. We drove through the small towns where the coal mines were shut down. The miners were standing around on the streets. I went up to a group and asked: "What's going on here? Why aren't you working?" J., himself a former miner, turned on me: "What's the matter with you, Walter? You *know* why they're not working." "I don't know anything," I told him. "I'm here to find out. I want to ask and be told."

One of my early assignments took me to the Wilkes-Barre anthracite coal-mining area, where a strike was about to take place. It was a tense and complex situation: some of the miners were already out; a rank-and-file movement was spreading—both against the bosses and the union leadership. The strike was halting production at a time (1941) when the slogan was "everything for the war." I went to the coalpits to see what was going to happen.

The men were dressed for work, wearing their helmets and

carrying lunch pails. Nobody was taking the elevator down the shaft. When I walked into the washroom, no one was saying or doing anything, just sitting around. Finally one man got up and emptied his water bucket, then another. One by one all the men emptied their buckets and began to drift away from the shaft.

That was the way they voted to go out—with their feet and their emptied water buckets. I saw how tortured the men were—they were united as a group, but each was a divided person: Each had his own stake in the war, a son or a brother or a father in the army. None of them wanted to stop producing coal; yet they had deep grievances.

Miners work thousands of feet underground; more than any other workers they all depend on each other, have to help each other to stay alive. I could see the union not as an abstract organization but a life-and-death affair for each man. No lofty speeches; no spellbinding harangues. One man emptied his pail, then another, and another—nothing had to be said: the strike was on.

The miners were a key union in the labor movement at that time—what they did affected other unions. If they were not won over to a win-the-war position, and if means other than strikes weren't provided to settle their grievances, strikes might spread throughout the country. This remained a crucial struggle throughout the war.

I talked to some of the men. "Why are you going on strike?"

"We're not striking—just not working today. . . . Have you ever been down in the mines?"

Later, as I covered other mine strikes, the same question was asked me over and over again: "Let the President go down in the mines and see what it's like. Have you ever been down in the mines?"

Finally I did go down into a mine—a low-seam mine in West Virginia. The vein in this mine was only four feet high; the men had to work bent over or sitting down. I, too, remained bent over or squatting for a couple of hours. Just being there, bent double in the darkness, with the roar of a coal car going past and an occasional gleam from a lamp, was enough to make an hour seem like a long hard day's work.

When I got out, with my helmet, my face and clothes covered with coaldust, I looked like a miner—and I was closer to realizing how it felt to be one, and why the miners, from Spain to Japan, from France to Kentucky, have been the most militant section of the labor movement.

I did the best writing I could to try to present the human drama of the coal miners; to make them come alive to our readers—not as an economic entity, but as men.

Jukebox in the Coalfields

It's Rosefield Gardens, Richeyville, teen-age coke bar in this Appalachian coalfield. You dance here or not at all. Unless you are older and go to Bentleyville, and mix on the crowded floor where the Polka Dots are making jive and the admission is 85 cents at the door.

The girls come into the coke bar from the cold night with kerchiefs on their heads. They swish behind a partition and emerge with freshly fluffed hair, to the tunes of "St Louis Blues" or "Kisses Sweeter than Wine." And Bill steps off with Hannah, and Ed puts his cigarette aside. What does the jukebox say?

You will hear its song on winter avenues or where the wolves prowl on Rocky Mountain snows. It vibrates in the submerged ninth of icebergs floating down the Atlantic from the Spitzbergen side of the pole.

Drown Bill and Hannah in coke, pour coal dust over them like a shower bath—they will go down once, twice—but the third time you will find them coming up like Venus on a sea shell, singing and swaying away. There is no silence here, and the miners young and old have a language that draws black music from the earth and keeps the world in a singing boil.

It is within giant peripheries that choices of action protrude
like stalactites among the icy caverns of the mines. You
will not know the coal miner from a word, only in some
secret crevice of his blind will-to-be.

It was a continual battle, with myself and with others, to try and show in a labor and political newspaper the human side of the class struggle. During one strike, when Art, a young photographer, was traveling with me, we covered a Polish wedding in a tiny hamlet. We did a picture story as if we were covering a society marriage at the Plaza. We wanted to show that these working people—not the Main Liners—were the top of the world. Some of the party leaders in New York objected: "How can our paper show miners dancing in the middle of a strike?" But William Z. Foster said to me later, "Sure, they keep on living, getting married, even during a strike."

As I worked on each story, I asked myself: Who are these people? To go on strike is a terrible decision—the most fundamental action a worker can take: How is he going to keep his family alive without a paycheck? How can he keep them alive without striking for a better paycheck?

In each labor struggle, I was an eyewitness to the drama that was taking place. It changes the insides of people—nobody remains the same, including me. I began to feel, as well as to know, that the miners and steelworkers and other workers are the heart and hope of democracy—the men and women on whom our survival depended.

When there were strikes for hospitalization and pension plans, I visited hospitals, interviewed injured workers, did picture stories. I began to live vicariously the dangerous life manual workers face every day. I covered disasters—explosions, cave-ins.

I was sent to Harlan County, Kentucky, to cover a fire in a small mine the week after Christmas. I reached the mine face while the fire was still raging thousands of feet deep inside. Rescue teams were still going in—and coming out with bodies covered with tarpaulins on stretchers. In the cold rain I watched with the silent crowd of mothers, wives, children. Suddenly there was a terrible cry; I looked around to find out what it was. The photographers, who had been waiting for a break, were already across the hillside, taking pictures of a wife who had broken down when she heard that one of the men under a tarpaulin was her husband.

And so I continued writing elegies—not in verse but in prose, and not for a couple of hundred readers of privately printed poems in Paris, but for the hundred thousand readers the *Worker* had at that time. Here is one of those elegies:

The Heiress and the Miner

Death has taken two more lives at the Glen Alden Coal Company. One of the victims never saw a coal mine; the other spent his life in them.

Consider the first victim: Miss Mary Powers was a silent stockholder in the Glen Alden Coal Company. She died in a $30-a-day hotel suite in New York, where she had lived as a recluse for 25 years. She was in her late 60's, but she never applied for an old-age pension. Her fortune, inherited from her family, was estimated at $15 million.

On the same day Miss Powers died, Philip Mileski was struck by a string of empty coal cars in the Wilkes-Barre colliery of the Glen Alden Coal Co. He was killed instantly.

These two deceased components of the Glen Alden Coal Company are known to us only through their simultaneous deaths. It is therefore only through this aspect that we are able to balance the books.

We examine, first, their calendric coincidence. There, on the statistical scale, all men and women who die the same day appear alike.

They weigh the same, being pure number.

The general mortuary tables alone carry them as equals. Take away the same accidental day, and these two deaths differ—even statistically. Philip Mileski enters the Bulletin of Mine Bureau Fatalities where Miss Powers can never obtain a foothold.

It is only in the Glen Alden dividend books that certain mine fatalities were for years inscribed under her name, duly credited to her account, checks drawn and eventually cashed.

Yes, even on the statistical level we find Miss Powers and Philip Mileski lie interred in their separate ways. The checks that went to Miss Powers now go to another Powers, as when our Miss Powers inherited her sister's riches—like a perpetual-motion machine. In the dividend books, the Powers name appears eternal. Tomorrow some other death will be inscribed in the dividend books for the inheritor of Miss Powers' golden name.

But never for Philip Mileski: An eternal void separates him from Miss Powers, just as it did when they lived together, unknowingly, on the Glen Alden Mine. Some other Philip Mileski, with a different face and a different body will contribute to the list of one thousand fatalities a year to which mine owners add a *digit.*

The men whose lives were essential to the diamond chain of coal survive in the Mine Bureau Fatality Chart only as abstract numbers. Whereas, each Miss Powers inherits and retains her unique identity through a specific dividend form, each check being payable to a specific man or woman for the shares of the general earth they own.

But as long as men have spades and machines and eyes to see, some one will know that Philip Mileski was here and changed the configuration of the earth's strata through the sweat and labor of his body. He is destined to be transformed, independent of his will, into magical shapes nobody can foresee.

That is his last testament and incontestable song—guaranteed not by banks and dividends, but by the deeds to come which all mankind must perform to live on any scale at all.

So, my education continued—in the coal mines, around the steel mills, in shops where I had never worked a day, at union conventions I covered as a reporter and never as a delegate. One of my friends was a local officer and a delegate to a steel convention after the war. I met with him privately before the convention, urged him to take the floor and speak out against the Marshall Plan that Philip Murray and other union leaders favored.

"Walter, I can't do it," he said at the end of all my arguments about peace and the Cold War, "they'll chop my head off. You don't know what it's like in that steel mill. You don't face the president of the steel company a few hundred miles away; you feel the foreman on your back. There's no exploitation like a steel mill, and there's nothing to fight it with except the union. If I take the floor against Murray, it will seem like an attack on the union. It's not only the diehards that would go for my scalp; I'd never be reelected to an office in my local. I'll be out as a force in the union."

Thus the correct theory of fighting against the Marshall Plan and the Cold War on the union floor came up against the bread-and-butter issues facing this steelworker in the shops. I learned how a policy that may be right on paper and for the long range may not be able to get support in the immediate situation in which workers find themselves.

I got a close-up on my own limitations as an intellectual without shop and union experience and began to understand why intellectuals cannot be the basic revolutionary group. In our society they can always find alternatives that enable them to survive: They can sell books, paint houses, manipulate here or there. The miners and steelworkers don't have alternatives; they must survive on the job. In that struggle, men are steeled to fight for change in the social structure.

It was during this period that I acquired a firm base for my political convictions. I realized from my own experiences in many struggles that there are no ideal solutions. Instead of taking my views solely from books and theories of how things should be, I learned how theories develop out of struggles that people have to engage in to stay alive. In one of my trips to Pittsburgh to cover a strike, I wrote:

Steel

In the end Patrick O. Landrino's name made the financial page. The passing of this young Duquesne steel worker occupied a paragraph on page 35 of the *Pittsburgh Press*.

By the merest chance, his death coincided with the annual financial statement of his employer, the U.S. Steel Corporation.

Though they occupy the same page, Patrick O. Landrino is inconspicuous at the bottom of the sheet. You will not find him posted above, among the imposing figures of the world's largest steel producer. He is not named in the extra dividends. He occupies no place in the "accelerated depreciation."

Patrick Landrino lived in the rear of 52 North Second Street, on the hills of Duquesne, where he worked for U.S. Steel. He left behind a wife and a five-week-old child. They saw him last when he went to work one day.

There was no body—no funeral in the ordinary sense. The coroner was given the following items: (1) A charred receipt; (2) a photograph; (3) a piece of leather jacket—all three were found in a flue for catching smoke at a blast furnace. To these were added the following facts: Patrick O. Landrino worked at this furnace. He was missing.

The furnace temperature is estimated at 3,000 degrees fahrenheit. The coroner concluded that he had been consumed inside the steel furnace where he had worked. There Patrick Landrino joined the anonymity of the steel ingots he helped produce.

Iron ore from the Michigan range; metallurgical opal from West Virginia mines; scrap from ploughs and tractors that farmed the wheat on North Dakota and Nebraska plains; the paper and manganese—all these earthly elements that workers pour into the U.S. Steel furnace from the four corners of the globe to make steel, have become as one with the body of Patrick O. Landrino.

Four billion years ago the earth began to lay down its store of carboniferous deposits out of which steel is now made. A grand geologic future beckons us ahead. Some will stay with the slow evolution of the earth's crust and live on in somebody else's name. When the last star spills over the Milky Way, U.S. Steel dividends will be dead to astronomy, as they have become a dead-weight, free rider on this spinning globe.

Patrick O. Landrino assumes a different shape. His frame and muscle vibrate in a steel girder that holds up a part of the building of the world. His pains, his hopes, his dreams of tomorrow have completely vanished. Only his life-work remains and cries out in some anonymous steel tube: "Remember me! Remember me!"

Shoes That Walked For Willie McGee

The appearance of the *Worker*, week after week, was a triumph over obstacles—money, indifference, competition with other objectives in the Party—that only the final ounce of persistence could overcome. It's not like editing any other paper; I couldn't just sit there and edit. There were no "think rooms," as they used to call the editorial offices of the *Philadelphia Inquirer*. I had to be on the front line every minute fighting in every way along with others to keep the paper alive. I helped to struggle within the Party to win support for the paper, to help get people to contribute money, or time and energy to sell it. I was directly involved in many of the civic, labor, racial or election issues in which the paper was involved—and I attended meetings!

Much of my life consisted of meetings: a meeting is called and its upshot is to decide to have another meeting. One of the miracles of the paper's continued appearance was the meetings it survived.

During much of this period, incidentally, I was on half-pay from the paper; and I was dedicating what was left of my shoe leather to selling intercommunication systems door-to-door to augment Lillian's salary from teaching—our basic support.

Working on the paper I had the feeling I was doing what I could to help shape the development of events—the election of a mayor, or better housing, or the campaign for a Second Front, or winning mass support to draft Roosevelt for a fourth term.

There were painful and rough experiences—I didn't come

through without scars, but I survived, and learned. I learned to do everything that I, personally, could do at a given moment. I learned to move around obstacles to gain what seemed to be the major objectives. I was part of a political organization, and I learned to deal with many people on many levels.

We were faced with complicated problems that would have baffled Spinoza—to say nothing of Marx. Often, because of the pressures of the moment or from force of habit, the wrong decisions were made. Then I had to learn, along with everyone else, how to correct errors. Every change in world relationships, every economic conflict had its repercussions in interior Party life. People on the outside haven't the slightest concept of what it is really like—thus, they don't really grasp the significance of why some people crack up. "You have to be made of iron," was my frequent grim thought.

Many of the major campaigns in which I was involved failed. One of my young associates on the paper once asked me after an election in which our side lost, "When do we stop winning the analysis and begin to win the election?" What could I answer but to quote: "The working class loses every battle but the last."

A heartbreaker was the campaign to save the lives of seven Negroes of Martinsville, Virginia, sentenced to be executed on the charge of "rape." I worked night and day on that one. Meetings, speeches, telephone calls: "Wire the President to stop the executions! Wire the Governor!"

A few days before the execution, I told myself I had done everything I could do to involve people. There was nothing left but to use my own feet. I went to Washington and became part of the picket line that marched back and forth in front of the White House. . . .

We made music that day—not with flute and violins—
    our feet in the February snow
slushed the blues

in front of the White House—
Mrs. Grayson at our head
one child in arms,
four at her side,
uttering her long, low song:
"I am a Negro mother. My husband is innocent.
Don't let them kill the father of my five
children. Don't let them kill the Martinsville Seven. . . ."

We made music, not over the Voice of America
but with Mrs. Grayson
her eyes tightening shut and her dark face
settling like an Aztec mask as her body drooped
and the hour passed
and the last sound parted from her lips
like a heartbeat ripped out of the
living sacrifice in the temple stones of America. . . .

They didn't execute them at once. I was in contact with other Washington reporters. In an interlude between executions, we went to the hotel where a Supreme Court justice was staying; he was deciding on a last-minute appeal. . . . We stayed up most of the night; finally the word came: No stay. . . .

A few days later, back in Philadelphia, I wrote my friends Pete Seeger and Lee Hays:

During the last hours of the night of February 1, when Rob and I were in Washington, concerned with the last unavailing efforts to stop the execution of the first four of the Martinsville Seven, we found ourselves talking off and on about Hazlitt, the English critic; about criticism in general, and about Rob's novel.

These conversations took place intermittently in taxis, as we tried to track down Supreme Court Justice Vinson; or waited in the hotel lobby while the attorneys pleaded, without success, in Justice Vinson's apartment; and while I was seeing Rob off on the bus for Richmond, the scene of the executions.

I don't remember the conversations in detail, but the subject of cultural criticism remains in my mind as a recurrent counterpoint to the action we were involved in, which we felt—as the minutes ticked off and the executions drew nearer—to be the knife edge of the universe.

This comes to mind now because I am writing while the minutes are again ticking off the eighth Negro to be executed in two months—Willie McGee. And again my mind, in the midst of life-and-death matters, turns to questions that concern art and the artist.

I am reminded that when Steve showed up unexpectedly last Thursday morning and we had a number of practical matters to attend to, the first thing we discussed was art and poetry and criticism, and he insisted on seeing all the Siqueiros reproductions I had.

And you will recall that in his last hours (Nietzsche points this out) while Socrates was drinking the hemlock, he called for writing materials, to record some poetry and music.

"The ultimate end of criticism," says Coleridge, "is much more to establish the principles of writing than to furnish rules on how to pass judgment on what has been written by others." And he adds, "if indeed it were possible that the two could be separated."

Coleridge's *Biographia Literaria* was in my pocket when I went to Washington, and that led to the discussion on criticism with Rob. This book is quite unlike criticism as we generally think of it.

Coleridge's criticism is not "pure"; it is shot through with his own life experiences. Arthur Symons says of it in an introduction to the Everyman edition, "The *Biographia Literaria* is the greatest book of criticism in English and one of the most annoying books in any language."

He goes on to say: "The thought of Coleridge has to be pursued across stones, ditches, and morasses; with haste, lingering and disappointment; it turns back, loses itself, fetches wide circuits, and comes to no visible end. But you must follow it step by step; and, if you are ceaselessly attentive, you will be ceaselessly rewarded."

I confirm this with a passage from the *Biographia;*

"I have laid too many eggs in the hot sands of this wilderness, the world, with ostrich carelessness and ostrich oblivion. The greater part indeed have been trod under foot and are forgotten; but yet no small number have crept forth into life, some to furnish feathers for the caps of others, and still more to plume the shafts in the quivers of my enemies, of them that unprovoked have lain in wait against my soul."

It is commonplace to say that a poet's life is in his poems—but much of mine is not. It remains unwritten alongside that of others who didn't record their particular share in the campaigns of which I, too, was a part. For example, the one to save Willie McGee from being executed:

Shoes that Walked for Willie McGee

I just ran across a pair of old shoes in a closet—shoes I walked in, picketing the White House for Willie McGee.

The story begins in 1945. Our soldiers were coming home from the allied victory in the war. One of them was Willie McGee, truck driver of Laurel, Mississippi.

In Laurel, the Masonite Corporation had its biggest woodworking plant. Its 3,000 workers had the strongest local in the union and the best conditions.

In November 1945, a white woman Willie McGee had known for years cried "Rape!" The first jury deliberated two-and-a-half minutes, with a white mob howling outside.

Now this case was fought through the courts for five years and was made known throughout the land. "Free Willie McGee!"

Inside the plant, the workers split—white and black. A strike was broken. Wages and working conditions went down.

The Jackson, Mississippi, Rebel Report Program broadcast

over Station WRBC the song: "Willie McGee will not be free."

In his death cell, Willie McGee wrote: "They are going to take my life to keep the Negro down in the South. Keep on fighting."

Five years we marched, paraded, assembled, sang, crusaded into Mississippi itself; chained ourselves to Abe Lincoln's pillars in Washington, picketed the White House. . . .

The 49 cops I count on motorcycles, patrol wagons, or just arms-akimbo on our pavement, look at their watches to see if they're hungry.

The 11 FBI photographers take the same pictures of us picketing in the May sun.

My dear shoes—do you think our walk was just a death walk? Do you know it's greener, that stone pavement, than the grass on the White House lawn? So soft, this pavement, so loving and soft to someone who will be walking for a long time.

His last words: "I have everything fixed up all right. I am ready to go."

And you, white America, do you have everything fixed up all right?

Are you ready to go?

He was the 44th Negro killed for rape in a state where no white man has ever been executed for this charge.

But it took the whole government of the United States to do it, and the whole world knew it.

In Afghanistan, Peru, Peking, Moscow, Paris, they knew it. And we knew it. In Mississippi, New York, San Francisco, we knew it.

And our anger—a patient earthquake rumbling faintly before it breaks.

And you, Laurel, sacred plant of the ancients with which they announced the victors in battle:

Let one fresh leaf shine for this worker of Laurel, Mississippi, for whose life we fought so hard because it meant so much.

On Trial

To Lee Hays, (on my return from jail) August 11, 1954:

It would be pleasant to be known as the typist who shared the universe with Eugene Debs, Prokofiev, W. C. Handy, and the moon.

I'm afraid we will all be lumped together as the Sun-Agers, people who lived when there used to be a place with planets, at $X41^{nnn}$.

Even the astronomer who invented this whole Sun-Age myth is going to glory with the be's and the not-be's.

And grammar, which we think so godly, will not spell out our good intentions.

Now I must add to the stellar dust: some son-of-a-bitch has been at my desk. I can see the traces–the paper shortage, the envelope addressed to a stranger, someone else's stain on my blotter.

People are relentless–like the sea. That's what happens when a person disappears–the rest of humanity just walks in and takes over.

Soon they will look back and wonder: what was the name of that fellow who beat it without a trace and left a typewriter behind?

I was sitting at my desk in the enclosed porch of our cottage in the woods, working on a poem. Suddenly floodlights and shouts broke through the darkness and the silence. Eight men pointing revolvers converged on my typewriter as if it were a machine-gun emplacement. It was 2 A.M., July 23, 1953.

It was a most successful raid; I haven't yet recovered from the surprise. In the years that followed, I was never even able to figure out what the FBI expected to find. If they were arresting me for my sonnets, I might have understood, and so might others. But for editing the *Pennsylvania Worker*? For sitting through hundreds of meetings? The Department of Justice should have advanced bearing medals, not guns.

Under steely-eyed surveillance I was told to put my clothes on. Lillian, in a state of shock, handed me shorts and socks, insisted over and over again she must make some coffee. She was to be left alone to live out this nightmare with the deer and the rabbits—the only fellow conspirators in our immediate neighborhood.

They let me bring one book with me. *Leaves of Grass* kept my mind off the proceedings that followed. I was taken to a building in Philadelphia that houses the FBI—along with other Philadelphians under similar custody. About 6 A.M. six of us were taken before a commissioner and each held in $100,000 bail. Never before or since in the United States have I been held in such esteem.

A large part of my adult life has been spent trying to overthrow not only the government but the universe. I thought I had the ideal weapon—the word. That's the way it all began, according to a respected source. In any just society a criminal like me would be judged on the efficacy of his weapons—in my case, poems.

Instead, I and my fellow defendants were tried for somebody else's words—and not words in poems, either. The words used against us at our trial were prose passages from Karl Marx and his descendants. The prosecution, fortunately, didn't quote the poems Marx wrote in his youth. They didn't even cite Lenin's observations about a period in the 1880's when, he said, all poets were socialists and all socialists were poets; they chose, rather, passages from *State and Revolution*, as interpreted by FBI Marxists.

Let me not underestimate the honor of being formally charged with serious opposition to the existing order. I am proud to be placed in the company of the best people—from Chu Yuan and Socrates to Dante and Kenyatta. If the higher courts, who eventually freed me and my friends, had studied Emerson, they might never have released me "for lack of evidence." The Sage of Concord warned: Beware of poets, they leave nothing unchanged; they overturn everything.

After my arrest, some of my relatives were worried—they thought there might be "repercussions"—that our neighbors might march on us. This alarm proved naive. In our South Jersey pine barrens, where deer are plentiful (even out of season) and an occasional moonshine still is not a completely unraided event, my arrest hardly made a ripple. Our neighbor who was interviewed in the local paper told the reporter: "He always paid for the eggs he bought from me." Johnny N., who lives down the road, told me after I returned from prison on bail: "Say, I heard they came and got you. I didn't know a thing about it until the other day at the sawmill; Jack told me. 'Johnny,' he said, 'they come and got your neighbor.' " In our area, people seemed to put "overthrow of the government" in the same category as moonshine or illegal deer.

One of the highlights of my trial never got into the court record. Because of my health—I had suffered a slight heart attack a few years before this—the judge allowed me to be excused early in both the morning and afternoon sessions, so that most days I spent only two hours in court. The rest of each day I wrote and read and rested at the home of friends who lived nearby. Both husband and wife were away all day working, so I had the run of their apartment, including their collection of records. It was here that I got an intensive education in Thelonius Monk, Charlie Parker, Charlie Mingus, Errol Garner, and other masters of modern sounds.

Another of my activities during the trial that the government did not include in its summation to the jury was the translation I did during the courtroom sessions. In all our years abroad, while I was being influenced by French and Italian poets, I had never translated any of them. It took 25 years and a tedious trial to get me started on this project. A friend of mine with long experience in courtroom procedures had advised me not to get bogged down in the legal verbiage. Since I found it hard to work on my own poems in the courtroom, I developed a routine—I wrote verse on my own time and translations on the government's.

Before our trial we nine defendants—the original group of six had been augmented—got together to discuss and decide our trial strategy. When my turn came to speak, I said: "Comrades, I have made many mistakes during my years in the Party. Some were left sectarian; others were right opportunist. During this trial of ours, I want to be sure all my errors are straight down the middle."

So it was unanimously agreed that my best contribution to our defense was to write poems. When I asked my comrades —not only in Philadelphia but in New York: "What can I do to help?" they would tell me: "Just keep on doing what you are doing—poetry and more of it."

Meanwhile, we served a few weeks in jail before our bail was reduced from $100,000 to $10,000, and I kept a record:

Our jail from an air view would seem a starfish spread on the ground; hump in the middle where our watch-tower sits, claws reaching out where the cell-blocks extend.

Inside we live an oceanic life—each of us submerged in his particular kind of crime: dope, robbery, murder, or, in our case, peace.

Each fellow-prisoner seems an ordinary man. "What are you in for?" I ask a 19-year-old, fresh, dimpled, smooth face. His mouth tightens, still smiling, purrs with a bite: "For not minding my own business, Mac."

We have no pedigrees here. We are all ciphers, numbers, mouths to feed, halls to scrub, cells to guard. Whatever our crime, the thing we share most intimately is: waiting to get out.

In jail there are two kinds of people—insiders and outsiders. Guilt or innocence, assault or robbery, frame-ups or caught-in-the-act—we all have one goal: to get out.

When I and my companions went to court for a hearing,

our cellmates would look at us wistfully. It was a change in the routine—a vicarious trip outside for them.

On our return, they'd ask in whispers, "How'd you make out?" . . .

> The murderer across the corridor
> is my own age.
> I never see his full face
> just his panther figure
> pacing his cell
> stopping to clutch bars
> becoming a hawk with hands
> gripping the false
> shelter of a nest
> he can't fly from.

To those on the outside, jail may have larger implications. Inside, it's the small things that count: the letters, meals, visits; the ventilator in the ceiling where a patch of light comes through. You become something that is acted on, rather than a man capable of acting with and upon others.

What is new here is the loudspeaker. Our prison apparently has Johnny Ray in permanent custody. Occasionally, the system announced orders from headquarters; the rest of the time—morning till late at night—it blasts a program of the louder pop songs.

In our block, the volume is particularly magnified. I hit on a pain-reliever—also a way of using my surplus bread. You have to eat whatever you get; no food can be returned. I learned to roll the excess bread into pellets for the ear-drums. The radio goes on even after lights are out, so I fall asleep with bread pellets soothing my ears. The moment of relief arrives; the radio is at last switched off. I wake up, remove the bread and enjoy the silence. In the heavy prison silence, I get up, crouch by the bars for light, and make notes:

What will you make of our generation 500 years from now, you unborn children? Only the other day I saw you in reverse. It was in the library; I was fingering Leonardo's volumes–great vellumed tomes two feet tall, the Italian master's notebooks, written before Columbus sailed. ("The supreme misfortune," I read, "is when theory outstrips performance. . . .") Here in my own hand, I held the drawings of airplanes, pumps, hydraulic machines, myriad engines of peace and war. And over the margins of the notebooks ("I can also paint," one note read), drawn in the master's own hand: human beings of all kinds–young, old, gnarled, grotesque; others bright with the warmth of the Florentine sun. And here in one man's work a whole generation came to light: their enemies, their loves, the truth and wisdom of their age–though their million, million names remain unsigned. . . .

Today I thought of Prokofiev–not only his music, his piano playing (I heard him play in New York in the early 20's); I recall his tall, thin, right-angled figure at the piano–blond, sharp, inscrutable, chipping off staccatos like feathered ice. I never heard him play as well as here in jail.

Being alone most of the time, I allow my mind to take the trips I can't make with my feet. I visit Emily Dickinson and understand her New England tartness better than ever before; walk down the streets of Homestead, Pennsylvania, and read the tribute to the martyrs of the 1886 steel strike.

One of the musicians who comes back to play for me is unknown today–only the old-timers will recall De Pachman, master of the velvet touch, brushing over keys like no one before him or since. De Pachman, talking to himself as he played, or, half-mad, it seems to us, accompanying his Chopin filigree. "Can anyone really be doing this?" "Did you ever hear such pianissimo?" All the while the music sifted from his hands as if from a separate keyboard. Only now in jail I begin to understand De Pachman's pride in his fingers' miraculous power: the notes, the melody, as given, barren, bare; the artist's touch so ardently mastered, all.

More details: We are each confined in a roomy cell, clean and airy, with a skylight, running water, toilet. The food is ample, though starchy. We are able to order newspapers, cookies, candies, and other extra extravagances available through the commissary. The treatment is not rough. Our cells are in a "maximum security" division of the Holmsburg County Prison.

We are kept to ourselves; we do not share the routine of other prisoners. We are fed in our cells; we exercise by ourselves in a large courtyard. This is the only time we can talk together except by shouting—mostly wisecracks—from cell to cell. Nothing extraordinary—only that we are behind bars until we can get out on bail.

Here in the dark, who dreams of murder? of rape? of robbery? Our dreams share the common poetry of aspiration: to be what we want to be, each with a life of his own. It is this dream I have been trying to get down in black-and-white for years. Not the dream of me alone nor any of us alone, but all of us together, when our stained clothing falls from us, and we stand naked before ourselves with the truth we are dreaming.

Today a tiny vent in my cell ceiling
sifts
a sunshower on my head
Electric fizz
of summer rain. I look up
and see
the atomic wonder of the universe—
the sun.
Right here in Holmsburg jail.
it slants
a ray on me. I might even get
sunburned
if the sun would only
stand still.

Our trial endured four-and-a-half months—a dreary time during which, as I have said, I spent as much time as I could reading and writing, in court and out, and studying the poetry of other writers in many languages.

The witnesses the prosecution put on the stand against us were former Communists who had become informers and agents for the FBI at a fair rate of pay. They testified about meetings they had attended, who was present, and what was *really* meant by what had been said. Their smoothest fabrications couldn't overcome the dullness of their narratives. It is hard enough to understand dialectics and how social changes take place throughout history, and what Marx and Engels and Lenin really meant. In the verbiage of the witnessess, Marxist thought and terminology became such a long-drawn-out gobbledegook of "proletariat," "cadres," etc., that I turned to Ben W., one of my co-defendants, one day and observed: "This jury is going to find us guilty of having endured boredom and convict us of talking nonsense." And so they did.

We were sentenced to jail; my term was two years, of which I served none. The Smith Act convictions in Philadelphia just happened to be among those reversed by the higher courts "for lack of evidence," although the evidence was as material or immaterial as that for which many others have served from three to eight years in prison.

The four years between my arrest and final exoneration I call my "jail period." Yet I actually spent less than a month behind bars. The rest of the time I was at liberty but under constraint. I was allowed to travel, if the court granted permission. Lillian and I even made one coast-to-coast trip, during which I read poems and helped spread the word about our case and collected some funds toward our defense.

There have been thousands of political prisoners in the United States. My experience before the Bar of Justice has only one unique feature: I was the only poet in recent times deemed worthy of being put on trial for my beliefs.

An anthologist has estimated that there are 400,000 poets in the United States. Each one of them has been judged by at least one critic to be "the outstanding poet of his generation." I am the only one with a court record and conviction to prove I am really dangerous. What an indictment of our craft! *

Speech to the Court

When the prosecution wheeled out cartloads of books to introduce at our trial, I expected some of my own words to be included along with the many quotations from Marx, Engels, Lenin, etc.

Of the half-million words that I have published in prose and verse during the past 30 years, not one was brought in as evidence to show "a conspiracy to teach and advocate the overthrow of the government by force and violence." This inability of the prosecution to cite any word of mine to support their case from all my published work—in the *Daily Worker* or in books of poetry—strikes me as an indictment of the case against all nine of us.

It might be said that the administration did not put me on trial as a poet or journalist, but only as a member of a "Communist conspiracy," as editor of the Pennsylvania edition of the *Daily Worker*. Who would believe that a poet is a poet when he writes a poem on Monday—but not on Tuesday, in the campaign to elect a decent city administration, and not on Wednesday, when he strives to obtain justice for a Negro falsely accused of murder?

People have a right to expect that poets shall be found wherever the common good is at stake. They have a right to expect more from poets than from others—precisely because poets are workers in the field of double vision, showing us not only the rose that is here today and gone tomorrow, but the one that endures.

It is sometimes said nowadays that a poet should not take sides, should not speak as a member of a political party. Poets have always taken sides; they are, as Hazlitt observed,

* This was written of course before the Montgomery bus boycott and the entire Movement that followed—during which anyone who is anybody has been jailed.

"naturally on the people's side" and "stay with us while they are worth keeping." From Dante and the Chinese master, Chu Yuan, who lived 300 BC, to our Whitman, partisan poets are the backbone of my craft. We do not by any means claim all the poets—a host of versifiers who oppose our views could be cited.

As for myself, I am not a poet despite my political convictions; it is my political convictions that are the final cement in my lifework as a poet.

It is not some abstract idea of freedom that poets whose tradition we follow have spoken for. Questions of war and peace, life or death for millions, national salvation or national suicide—these are the issues at stake in the right to speak.

It is, I hold, resistance to tyranny that gives the true temper of any period and measures its lifeblood. To a world that has from the very beginning known the hard price of freedom, our land has for generations stood as a "torch, a flame, a Mother of Exiles." The poem of Emma Lazarus still spells it out on the Statue of Liberty: "Give me your tired, your poor, your huddled masses yearning to breathe free. . . ."

Was it ever a free gift? Isn't liberty, as Emerson said, constantly slipping from those who boast it to those who fight for it?

Now we are past the age of martyrdom. We are in the new era when the heritage of the world is to be enjoyed—not by a handful of privileged persons, but by all the people. This period we are going through in the United States is a painful hangover of an epoch that is already vanishing—a time when people were jailed, or had to fight against being jailed, for their beliefs.

The stoolpigeon, the informer, the *agent provocateur*, the H-bomb psychotic—these can still hold forth on the front pages of the newspapers. The true America holds out its hand to hundreds of millions of friends throughout the world. It speaks clearly in the music, poems, histories, novels, pictures, dances, sagas of the great legion of free speakers who are speaking out in our land today.

They are the voice of a movement to resist suppression of thought and speech. They speak, consciously or unconsciously, for the majority of our people, the working people of the United States, the nerve center and backbone of our democratic vision. They are representative of the real America—the true "Colossus of the North"—and they are in a creative upsurge that cannot be stopped.

There is nothing new in repression—it has been going on since Tiglath-Pileser, Assyrian tyrant of 1100 BC, ordered the jawbones removed from poets who displeased him. What is eternally fresh is the *Divine Comedy* that Dante wrote in exile; the poems of Shelley and Heine, Hugo, García Lorca (Franco had him murdered); Brecht and Becher, poets of the German resistance; and all the great legion of the free speakers of the past who could not be silenced. . . .

"As good almost kill a man as kill a good book," said Milton. How can the law prevent books from speaking? To keep my voice silent, wouldn't it be necessary to jail all my books? to destroy every poem I ever wrote? And not only my books, but the works of all poets on the side of freedom? For they also speak for me, even though they do not mention my name. What is at stake in this court is not so much the jailing of a poet and his right to speak, but the right of people to read and to listen. This right the people will never give up.

Poetry is my "crime"—the poems that go into and out of words, the poems of laughing children, of young men and women who know what tomorrow will bring—all those living poems that cannot be destroyed: the poetry of human endeavor, of people who ask only to live in peace and brotherhood, of man's destiny to triumph over all inhuman things; I speak here not for the poetry of a single poet, nor any group of thousands of poets, but the poetry of humanity entire.

To Pete Seeger, folksinger and composer, August 27, 1953:

I have a map engraved in my mind—it is of my nine counties,

the nine counties that make up the Eastern Federal District where I am confined by bail—some beautiful places there, Schuylkill County in the lower anthracite, Pocono Mountains, Delaware Water Gap. . . .

Last winter before we bought our Weymouth shack we thought of taking a trip to Cuba in connection with some studies I was making of Latin American poetry. We thought also of some day visiting Martinique, to talk with Dr. Aimé Cesaire, one of the leading French poets. I thought surely some day we would get to the little town of Chillan, in Chile, where one of Siquieros' masterpieces is on the walls of a school—a mural, "Death to the Invaders."

Even then we had about given up the idea that we would ever again have the time, or strength, to make another walking trip up the Seine and retrace our footsteps of 1932. When we bought the Weymouth cabin, we also said goodbye to Chile, goodbye to Cuba, and to China.

At last, after all these years of moving around in other peoples' houses, we were "settling down," not the Dream House, not the Dream Trip, but the place we could actually afford and manage with the strength and funds and obligations at our command.

I don't know whether we had a premonition, but we concentrated in getting a few minimum things done to make it liveable quickly, a bathroom, a porch extension to make a third room, finding nearby workmen, buying the material—it was just about getting finished the last week of July. We had made final payment to our carpenter, still had painting to do, but the kitchen paneling was up, and the bookshelves in, when—presto! I was arrested. Even Weymouth was out of reach, and now that I am out on bail, it is out of bounds.

Michelangelo painted on the ceiling and wall of the Sistine Chapel his great apotheosis, but the things that never get painted are the small insignificant human sights that pass before your mind's eye in jail . . . the flower market near the Duomo in Florence, where we lived in 1926. . . . I never saw the Duomo so clearly. It was early in the morning, 5 A.M. by my watch, I could smell the cornflowers right in jail, and touch their blue fringes.

David, too, the Michelangelo statue in Florence without a fig leaf and with the American schoolgirls staring at him. . . . I went on a tour to the places I have known, Tunis, Paris, and wound up in the Amphitheatre in Rome with the voices at my shoulder, as they had been 30 years ago: "Want a guide? Want a guide?"

Now things are on a more practical basis; I am surrounded by concrete and tangible riches—nine huge counties; if I were an ant my confines would be the size of a galaxy, but as it is I feel I am in a strait jacket, and the only places that count are the ones where I cannot go—China, Chillan, and the little cabin we just finished in nearby Weymouth.

To Earl Robinson, composer, August 13, 1954:

There is one crime only a poet can commit; not to be a poet. This crime humanity does not forgive.

We expect Mozart to complete his Requiem on his deathbed. We demand from Beethoven the music of his deaf years. We expect poems from a poet, no matter where he is—transport, not persuasion.

To the wolf we are all Siberians, all smell alike. In a poem we are each unique, opening each morning the shutters of our sleep on new, familiar faces.

A poem measures the specific gravity of human beings against the pressure of their time; weighs how each gets on and off the universal scale as it moves from fossil footprints toward tomorrow's rockets.

It is sometimes thought that the age of prophecy is done. We are in the infancy of vision. The real process lies ahead: not to have "vision" but to live a visionary reality, the dream world come true, the aim and substance of our lives incarnate in the other person's warm embrace.

Some of us see this as a tragic age, with the individual denied. This defines the limits wherein our sense of history as a human process is confined.

I am in love with this Goddess of History—even as she drives her triumphant chariot over heaps of us. In her eye is the secret of the way the ball rolls. The slightest sibilance of her breath makes the tinsel mountains crumple—as we move on.

She whispers to every heart that can hear an old story never fully told: Behind her lies everything inert, vanquished, out of which human beings of tomorrow arise; the song that counts is the one that hears even in the beginning, the end; the only tragedy is not living the fulfillment of our age. —*Holmsburg Prison, Philadelphia*

The scene opens at my desk, in our small house in the woods. In the typewriter are notes concerning translations that I wrote during our Smith Act trial. The telephone rings. Philadelphia is calling.

It is my co-defendant, Joe Roberts.

"You won't be able to write any more poems from prison. The government has asked the Court of Appeals to acquit you for lack of evidence."

The scene proceeds then as follows:

I congratulate Joe. I kiss Lillian. I telephone my bailsman. I telephone my children.

It is a sunny fall afternoon. Lillian and I take a ride. In the South Jersey woods where we live, the sun seems trapped in the leaves of the oaks, maples, ash.

Comes the Mystery Question: "What are you going to do about being free?"

"I don't know. What do you think I should do?"

"You have two choices: You can issue a political statement, saying it's a victory for the country, for peace, for the Bill of Rights, for the working class, and so on.

"Or you can say: 'I beat the rap.' Make it cool. Thank your mouthpiece, and all the others who helped. Happens every day. Innocent guy gets picked up on a bum rap, the Feds can't make it stick, and they gotta back out—all the way! Some of our neighbors might understand it better that way."

"You sound cynical, that's unlike you. Maybe it's just delayed shock. All of a heap you're being hit by what you had to go through the past four-and-a-half years. That's why you haven't mentioned my third choice."

"What's that?"

"To keep on writing. That's what I continued doing after I was arrested. In fact, I have a page in the typewriter at home which I should be finishing right now."

So we had a little Jersey beer to celebrate, and here I am, back at the machine.

I was getting ready, I started to say, to give you a sample of some of the translations I did during our Smith Act trial.

One sonnet I translated in court is by the French 19th-century poet, Baudelaire, from his book, *Flowers of Evil.* His sonnet about truth and beauty came in handy while the Department of Justice had some of its most unlovely fabricators on the witness stand.

BEAUTY

I am lovely, O mortals, like stone in a dream
and one by one you bruise your hands on my breast
made to inspire in poets love without rest—
eternal, speechless, pure as a light beam.

I am the sphynx of skies no one exhausts.
I am the heart of snow in a swan's plume,

I am the order in the humblest room
I never laugh nor cry in the bitterest frosts.

In austere studies, poets day by day
consume themselves for phrases to make sense
of what I've given to proud monuments,
and so I take their docile hearts away;

for I have mirror eyes where all things grow
more beautiful for the clarity I bestow.

Coda

To Nan Braymer, July 13, 1964:

I never gave up my belief in death. Perhaps that's the essential continuity between my years as a poet in Paris (1926-1934), then a reporter and editor of the *Daily Worker* (1938-1954), and thereafter my return to poems. There was a change, but the essential difference was in locating the source of the putrefaction and the life growing out of it. My integration to the working class and a Marxist outlook wasn't based on any temporary or fluctuating emotion or situation—such as unemployment, hunger, discrimination. I knew from my beginnings as a poet that we were surrounded in the United States by death. Later I found it was a world-wide disease, and cureable. No matter how the ups and downs of the struggle shook me, I was able to survive all the betrayals, disasters, defeats, because I had already taken as an irreducible fact the old world's disintegration, and I knew there was only one way out—a totally new social realignment. It wasn't any vision or illusion of the bright future by itself that made me a socialist, but the impossibility of living with the present. My belief in the future was indissolubly integrated with my personal rejection of the present social order. To stay alive, I was driven to find a way out of the graveyard toward which I saw our civilization headed.

Once I began to make the switch and joined in organizational actions around all sorts of immediate issues, strikes, civil rights, and so on, I had no need to write about my reasons. They were insignificant in the struggle.

It's not only that you can't step into the same waters twice, as Herakleitos told us, but you can't die in the same way twice, because death too is always changing. That is what

I started to document over 30 years ago when I started *Some Deaths* in Paris and even asked for a Guggenheim grant after the work was under way to research the change in burial customs—which struck me as one way of documenting the changing attitudes about death, the soul, graves. I went overboard on it and wrote "death is the moral force of the world," and that's the way I finally arrived at life—through death. My researches finally led me to Hegel and thence to Marx and the discovery that it wasn't "the world" *en tout* that was death to the creative process to which I was dedicated, but that layer of the world that dominates the northwestern hemisphere; I began attending rallies at the Salle Bullier on the Boulevard St. Michel, just a block away from where we lived on the rue Denfert Rochereau, turning toward the "real world" unconsciously and instinctively like a heliotropic plant. Remembering now the poster I saw in front of the hall of a rally to be held for the Scottsboro Boys, with a picture of one of the Scottsboro mothers, Mrs. Wright, I went to the meeting, stood in the back of the crowded hall and saw for the first time posters with slogans on them —"Free Ernest Thaelman" . . . "Free The Scottsboro Boys" . . . "For Peace and Socialism," . . . and heard dimly the speakers, not only Mrs. Wright but the French Communists of the day, whose names I forget and whose words I forget, but it stirred some curiosity in me in relation to the dead world of burials I was documenting, and I bought the pamphlets one buys at such meetings, one of which I still had until very recently—"Program of the Sixth International. . . ." And then, on leaving the meeting, the *flics* keeping us from marching in a demonstration, as had been planned, and beginning to beat the people on the fringes, we all had to run down the Boulevard and into side streets and, instead of walking the two blocks home, I was with the crowd running and scattering and hating the *flics* like everybody else and feeling that I too belonged "independent of the will" to the crowd who had been doing nothing worse than attending a meeting and marching afterward down the street with banners

"Free Ernest Thaelman" . . . "Free The Scottsboro Boys". . .

Perhaps I did know a trifle more about it than I can recall now, but if so, my work of the time doesn't show it. It was our feet that were in the right place and we—Lillian, too, although she was in her seventh month with the twins —were with the February crowds that marched toward the center of the city to demonstrate against the attempted Fascist putsch in 1934. But it was only long afterward that I really understood the "United Front" that was in the process of forming at the time. All we knew was where our hearts were and our feet.

So I reached the end of that death in Paris through a combination of research, frustration, and the fertility of death as subject; reading Marx about two classes, which I saw as the living and dead, "class war" carrying on the fertility rites of Dionysus I had been studying in the Bibliothèque Nationale . . . the death of winter, the birth of spring. . . .

> "we are the should-be's of the dead
> doomed to winter it among the squids
> in the ice-age of our make-believe."

And afterward the workers and the national liberation movements were not to me just a *ding an sich*—they were the "moral force of the world" without which death would rule forever and there was no fertility left except suicide. I haven't yet gotten to what I started to say this morning about the way death changes—but you can already see on this sheet as on many others how impossible it is for me to write about the Paris days in the usual terms of literary interest, people, gossip, names of writers—at any rate, except as periphery. I saved my life in Paris, in the streets, with the people, running from the *flics*, demonstrating in the February days, attending the rallies, beginning to read not just the "philosophy" of Marx but the way it was being acted out.

So if you wonder how it is I remained a socialist all my life thereafter, with all the geological pressure to which we all have been subjected, you can see that there is something to what Harold Rosenberg says, "O Walter, he belongs to a party all his own." Of course, the party of spring eternal and life everlasting against the long winter of the old God we are burying—not in the way we should, but in the only way we can.

Just as the rites of Dionysus change from ice age to ice age, and you no longer dance in the hills with the fawn men and the leaping women as you tear the bull to bits and devour the raw meat with its running blood, because that's the way you share the strength of the bull—so the death you live through, the one you anticipate one way or the other, via insurance, dreams, dreads, plans, burial plans, wills—that daily counterpoint to your living—is also changing all the time.

It isn't only the social attitudes and responses to death and burial that change—from Cro-Magnon man, cave paintings, totem poles, dance masks, and corn buried with you so you can make your way in the spirit world. Or the Etruscans who burned the corpses and put their ashes into beautifully carved urns that you can see to this day in the museum in Volterra, Italy.

Your personal death changes—from the far-off receding tracks where the train of death is waiting unobtrusively for the passengers who are getting there one way or another—straggling, running, jumping or even trying to run the other way.

My own aim is to arrive in whatever state I am—forgotten corpse or still lively body—with one or two representative and complete books that I won't be ashamed to show. I don't defend this approach of mine—I realize it is egocentric, narrow, without the world vision I should have for all humanity, but it happens to be the way I feel—racing the cardiogram I had taken yesterday to finish whatever messages I have—because with all my restrictions and limits I know there is a peculiar angle I get at times that nobody will ever finish if I don't. And that's the best present I can make to everyone: that with all the time I wasted and misspent, from peddling butter in New York and intercommunication systems in Philadelphia to the millions of words of crap on which I used up energy, I did wind up in my late 60's at the point where I should have been in my 30's—justifying my existence via the typewriter and my changing death—which is to say, my many lives.

To Francois Hugot, December 1, 1964:

This is the end, the final somersault, the last page. I am referring to the date—December first. It echoes a blast of snowed-in winter, with no logs in the house yet for the days when the electricity goes and we have only our candles and our fireplace. A taste of what we are all in for in the iceberg centuries. We can still escape by going south a few miles. But over-all, it's a losing game.

I'm not complaining. I am in love with geology. The sedimentary rocks give me a thrill. I know my death (like my life) is not alone. I love the earth for our common doom—and our mutual joy. We shall go out as we came in—together—and if one of us precedes the other by a billion years or two, what's that between eternal friends? I'm just a chip off the old block, and so are you, my friend, carrying your actions and inactions with you like the old man of the sea—I mean the one who rose from the galactic waters with the earth on his back.

2

Poetry

EDITOR'S INTRODUCTION

Much has been written and much more said about the poetry of Walter Lowenfels. His works have been widely translated and honored by major artists throughout the world, and he even gets an occasional royalty check from China. Not Formosa–China.

The fact is, he is known and honored least of all in his own homeland. Occasionally a mass circulation publication may admit his name to print, usually with a cop-out such as: Isn't it strange that a man who doesn't agree with our Demo-GOP politics and the way we divvy up our profits, that such a man is capable of poetry? One is left with the impression that many a literary critic might lose a good-paying gig if he came out loud and clear in praise of Walter's poetry, for it seems that most members of our literati *are more interested in pleasing certain monied interests, and have less courage in the face of fiscal dangers than most streetwalkers.*

Well, I'm not a literary critic. And, to lift a phrase from

Nelson Algren, "It's four minutes to midnight and a madman's at the wheel." Yes, it's too late now to even think of sweating that old McCarthy nightmare about "are you now or have you ever been?" Those fingers on the buttons have us on the eve of our extinction and certain of our fellow countrymen would rather be dead than anything else, it seems.

Of course there's still that one school of thought that proclaims the human race will manage to save itself from itself, and Walter belongs to this school. Personally, I'm a bit skeptical, but in the meantime, reading poetry can be an uplifting and enriching way to pass whatever time the button-fingers may grant us. I have been enriched by Walter's poetry, so I want to pass it on.

Now I pass it on to you not as an analyst of what are surely interesting innovations in style and technique, for these are the tools of the poet, not what he is making. What he is making is like furniture for the spirit; I like to fancy Walter's poetry as a place to rest a soul, a calm mid all the churning chaos of this life, a place to go to get oneself together. Because it radiates, in this day of nuclear fallout, a kind of antidote for the invisible particles of fear that are constantly eating at our God-given volition.

The beauty of Walter's outlook is that he confronts this permeating fear, these parasites of the individual spirit, head-on. And instead of choosing to escape their effects on him, he gives you what only a truly great poet can give you: a new and timeless perspective. He puts our nuclear predicament into its proper place in the larger scheme of things. He not only tells it like it is, he tells it like it always was and always will be. Instead of accumulating facts or impressions that add up to a lie, he employs fancies that aim your mind at a truth. He breathes life into deadly scientific structures and concepts, and he tells us where we're *at in time and space. And behind his telling of it, our earthly here-and-now concerns, our prejudices and our tiny high-rise ambitions are seen for what they are—tremendously absurd.*

R. G.

FROM *Some Deaths*

For Lillian

Let's get a bulldozer,
plough up every street we ever lived.
begin all over from scratch
as if it were the first day
we met and you were lame
but I never noticed
because you were so much you
and did everything your own way
anyhow.

Believe me it's not all gloomy
like when you're half-paralyzed
and showering is an agony
on a hard chair,
we can always rely
on doing it together—
you hold the shower rail
and I hold you
and what love
can be purer or cleaner
than going into the shower
hugging each other?
Just to stand up
and get soaped
clean to the end,
so happy you don't have to
wash alone in that cold
hospital chair.

So, as I said,
it's not all gloomy—
just a question of balance.
I love you
even though all I say is
"please pass the soap."

For My Daughter's 20th Birthday

You looked at me today
with such pity for my age,
I felt sorry for something—
I forget which.
My beautiful stranger,
let's face it—you
also are not the angel head
you came with twenty years ago.

What bothers me, my darling, is not age
but the aged.
To get a breath of fresh air
away from my generation
I visited my ancestors yesterday—
the dinosaurs
on the fourth floor of the museum.
I love the uselessness of these 100-foot memories;
they have nothing to say to me
and they have not been saying it
for eighty million years.

Pity the poor
dinosaur
He doesn't live here
anymore.

What a relief to be able to visit
 the age group under us!
(Consider the traffic jam
 if death didn't help rid us
 of these monsters—our dead selves.)

For my was-ness
I have no excuse—
 just an old buffalo head
lifting my snout on the crowded prairie
 of my generation;
not even suggesting that we hurry along
 or be anything other than we are.
I can cure everything but my age—a disease
 which follows me to the grave—
after which I convalesce.

Elegy for the Old Language

"Why have thirty American poets committed suicide since 1900?"
—Kenneth Rexroth

Language in the U.S.A. has become so disturbed,
 when a poet uses it for resonance-capture,
 everybody thinks his truth is lying—that makes people
 feel bad and they kill themselves.
In the solar mirror in which we live, the coroner
 thinks it is the poet who has committed suicide. . . .

Motivists speak of our weak character.
 Across the desert border,
 on the Aztec altar where
 we are all lovers in the flesh,

we watch those who escape the cyanide
    having their hearts ripped out.

Even the "earth" in "rare earth" is not completely descriptive.

On the high end of the verbal spectrum
where words are metal, you pour out like beads;
only a poem measures the optimum relationship,
unveiling the riddle of rolling friction in the
                magnetism of the sun.

Slice light the way you want it.
Where do we go from minus 320°F?
Magnetic exploration along the crystal axis?

Guided tour of the solar system?
Reaching tomorrow is our job;
    success is to survive as a turbulent
    transfer in the cybernetics of cre-
    ation–not a chopped, stabilized amplifier.

On this vertical oscillator radar tracking unit,
    lively as a walk on the moon,
from kitchen to stars,
    camera weds duplicator
    fishing for neutrons.
Cosmic butterfly
    spreading its wings
to absorb the eternal flow of solar energy.

In conclusion, comrade space,
The Big Elk is rounding the Cape of Good Hope.
    The horn is on the deer. Beyond magnetic memory
    bells are sounding in star spaces
    and the Dog mounts the Bear.

Are you ready to go? Do you know which way the
    microwave is moving?
Have you got the ice-cutter ready for the
    passage around Point Vega?
And he named me Antrium and I said: "You don't
    frighten me. I have been used to you for
    ten thousand years. You always tell the last
    tale and you never win the first story.
Cut out the chatter. The time has come to start
    the Big Journey and we are all ready."

Shield for the battle for survival in space;
electroluminescence;
plasma flame spray;
plumbing for posterity.

The Impossibilists

I saw the Impossibilists
    sustain a low-altitude satellite against drag,
    vary the eccentricity of its orbit,
    pinpoint its fixes by celestial navigation.

I saw airborne navigation systems
    listening to stars no telescope can see
        shape another sun.

I saw the Advertisers quoting, unquoting:
    "every cubic inch of space is a miracle,"
    "but war's a game which, were their subjects
        wise, kings would not play at";
asking:
    "Where do you stand in programming progress?"

I saw the Impossibilists looking at the measurement
of a billionth of a second,
tying molecules in knots,
announcing: "Today is obsolete."

I heard the electronic brain dictate:
"O Digital Telemeters of the world's most
quoted analogues:
what are your paddle wheel planetoids vaulting
through unexplored space,
if we lose the ray of hope from the atom?

"What are space probes,
slip grab stresses,
artificial neutrons—
if we are not earth creatures
turning our glacial spillways
into moon gardens?"

Every Poem Is a Love Poem

I am trying to break through this language to get to
fireboxes
Cooper-Bessemer compressors
magnetic films
without the copperbelt lining that keeps my hope
from exploding out of this typewriter,
desk, window, through the pines, down the
Little Egg Harbor River, across the
Continental Shelf.
"Reaching for ultimate simulation"
is an earthborn facility
where the almost limitless field
of space and electronic simulation

reproduces the condition of
roll
pitch
yaw
rotation
buffeting
all at various controlled speeds
of three-dimensional vibration.
(Engineers–check your answers and mail today–
pleasant living conditions
company stability & prestige
desirable fringe benefits such as
year-around recreational facilities, etc.)
and love
LOVE
L O V E
(also–more love)
And yet
what instrument will measure
on the moon
on the planets
many minds that work as one
(such as yours perhaps)
("somewhere you stand waiting for him")?

Through a column to a detector
in the form of burned-off gas
after an electric oven decomposes.
I am finished
with thrust deflection
secondary injections
cryogenics–
I rely only
on plastic sleeves
optical comparators
propulsion systems

and Slade's elastic band.
Otherwise I am lost
(don't stand there waiting for me!)
Missiles are thrusting farther with greater accuracy
"impossible" control jobs are becoming daily routine
when it comes to colonizing the moon—
the regenerative liquid metal cell
will replace
power steering
air breathing
and
Anyone for Mars?
to see to measure to know?
and to love
LOVE
L O V E?

From an Exposition of Power and Industrial Machinery

Open float inspirator and injector
super simplex pulverizer
gyrating cruster
armature spider
quick-change chuck and collet
clipper-belt lacer
expanding lathe mandrel
non-return vertical indicator
multiwhirl baffle
hanger boxes
pillar boxes
drop-forged steel body
hardened worms with thread ground
cement slurry
metallurgical slimes
carbon steel hand taps

precision high-speed ground thread taps
two and three fluted taps
spiral pointed serial hard machine screw
bent shank tapper taps
mud or washout spindle staybolt
couple taps for pipes and tubes
short die hobs
long die hobs for the man who
makes his own dies.

For Ludwig Wittgenstein

1889-1951

Playback from space:
Controlled power.

First comes the fire: this is the purification;
one in a billion survives the flame; he is
the Speaker.
Out of the agony of survival the word is born
that releases us.
The moment it is said we realize it is not a
word at all—this is what Wittgenstein
tried to explain.
It has been demonstrated that the temperature
near the stagnation point increases as you
approach the sun. This is the nodule of the
nexus.
We live on a tangent to the heat fix; the
possibilities of igniting are more than our
mathematics provide. This adds a continual
incentive to a more precise formulation of
the equation Wittgenstein was trying to
tell us just as he died.

For the foam of the future
fast-breeders
must know the sun better.

Good-Bye, Jargon

(Elegy for a small press)

Since 1492 some 175 million of us in the U.S.A. have
advanced from deserts, wastes, forests and lonesome prairie
to a thruway of cities, highways and missile bases, with
unemployed men and women on every corner.
There is still one practically uninhabited mountain pass
and that's the poetry-crossing over the Big Muddy.
Publish a book of poems in the Strontium Age and you can
enjoy all the rigors of striking out on a new Oregon Trail.
The rapids, the natives, the rain, the heat, the cold, the
thunder–they're all there–particularly the long lonesome
days and nights when you don't see a chipmunk reader
peering across the poetry route along the Columbia River
highway of your dreams.
When you consider there are 400,000 of us turning out the
stuff these days, and several hundred of us proclaimed the
"Greatest Poets of our Generation," you can realize what
a huge vacuum our non-readers are creating.
Do you wonder the earth is slipping on her axis and the moon
is a decimal off-center every other thousand years?
There aren't enough poetry readers turning pages
to keep the side-slip of our jet travel around the
universe on an even keel
We are slipping down the hydrogen side of the galactic spiral
with poems receding from our unreading eyes, and
everybody wonders can the next explosion save us from
smashing our lovely planet without even an elegy for its
good-bye.

In the great silence even Tiberius no longer asks what song
the sirens sang; what the Emperor of Today hears
is the mushroom screaming:
And that's the song.

Welcome Home to Cubby

Among the sixteen thousand insane inmates, he was the
conscious maniac. He doesn't want to be normal. He
can't stand the sexless odor of it.
Something happened to him—in the navy—in the army—
in the Red Hook dives of his Brooklyn underworld.
The lining of his country's stomach got turned inside out
for him and he saw what he could not swallow.
Some people say he's nothing but a dirty writer.
I hear the pin-drop of what he has lost unloading
its specimen over the Flatbush Avenue marshes.
Of course we can't stand it. It's our personal fall-out
trickling down the Gulf Stream. It's the crotch
of our Pentagon's cleanest H-bomb. It's the other
self we are trying to turn our back on—the corpse
of the old Dog-Eat-Dog lousing-up Rockefeller
Plaza years after it should have been laid out.
It's too late now for burial. It has to be cremated.
Meanwhile, to participate in the ceremony, Cubby
has himself to burn.
That hiccough laugh he gives as he talks and grabs for his
anti-allergy pills hasn't to do with anything funny.
He's allergic to the universe. He's looking for
everlasting love in the urinals. It's the acid drip
of human intercourse that's biting him. He is
working toward that one word that will drop us all
without an echo of his being alive alongside three
billion others for whom his desperation is the tombstone
they have to overturn if they are to survive.

Speech to the Court

Even now the question has changed since I started this
summation to the jury. How can we arrive at an honest
verdict? The crime consists in going on
trial in the first place.
We should all be declared innocent by birth.
You get the drift? You answer the question and I will
always find a new one and we will go arm in arm
down the airways singing Happy Birthdays.
But don't ask me to pull the Trujillo bullet from your brain,
the Nazi needle from your heart; put out the
White Citizens' fire toasting your feet or
extract the Strontium 90 from your bones.
Once we start that kind of business the bleeding begins
and we commit the unforgivable sentimentality—as if
a handcuff were latched to our fossil skins and
we grinned up at the anthropologist who discovered us
at the fireside where we were heartbeats loving each
other so sweetly in the kitchen middens we can't
forget.
We are not desperate—that passed with the first mushroom
when the Pentagon said to God: "Let there be
clouds" and we all started singing Peace.
It's not a choice between madness and suicide—
that's only the way it appears. The choice
historically is to be heard or not to be heard;
to accept the vast silence around us or to
scream intelligibly.
Just believe in sunshine up to the limits of your
benefits under the Unemployment System and you
will smile like bacon cracklings in the morning
happily forever after. . . .
—for our eyes see ahead
and we know we are moving
toward the songs of others.

Letter to Steve Nelson

Let's talk as we used to, Steve
not as in each other's prison
(am I on bail? are you inside?).
One hardly knows from day to day now
which of us is where . . .
Let's talk anyhow as we have so often
of that great mountain the world—
toss it back and forward
from prison to prison
as we used to with baseballs.
How is it with you?
Can you see the sky as I couldn't
in my jail a week or two ago?
The air itself begins to wear stripes.
The hills you visited me in once
now seem earthwide security walls
where the lights go out at starlight time
and the Monongehela is a moat around your darkness too
(telling us how much they fear
how much they cannot win!)
Did you see the ivy glisten in Hindustan this year?
Did you see the jonquils glow in Kenya?
Did you see the snow melt in the Bolivian uplands?
Did you see the edelweiss purpling—
yes on the high Pyrenees in Spain?
Did you smell the scent of victory
even in the gritty Pittsburgh smog?

We are partners in a worldwide array
everything according to schedule
a leeway here a lifetime there
in the long run everything on time.

You lead from strength—

2,000 million human beings including
Memphis, Tennessee. Even today
from the rent that haunts our sleep.
meat that costs too dear, pay check
that crumples, taxes that gnaw the bone
ten thousand times ten thousand
prisoners spring, carpenters too like you . . .
The builders move not with banners yet
but softly in the hushes of the dawn
where sleep wrestles with sleepless brows
and bills frown on wars that day may bring.
Thousands yes thousands think, dear Steve,
of *their* lives, just so
of us, especially of you
who wash so freshly the human name.

Giordano Bruno

In the year of Jubilee,
in the early morning
to the chanting of litanies
and the songs of the first birds:

Bruno
stripped by the servants of justice
bound to a stake
for a word . . .

"Only one bereft of reason could believe
those infinite spaces of the stars,
tenanted by vast and magnificent bodies,
are designed to give us light . . ."

How many years
were eight years
of a Roman dungeon
racks of the righteous

centuries of doubts
    to burn for a word? . . .

. . . "The earth is but a planet;
the ruler of our earth is not
man but the sun . . ."

Eyes crackling,
arms blackening
for drums and cheers, only
    Hold fast, Bruno!
from what inaudible voice?

"You who sentence me
are in greater fear
than I who am condemned."

Burnt alive for a word . . .

". . . who is more deeply moved
by the thought of some other thing
does not feel the pangs of death . . ."

So in our hearts he burns
a three-hundred-year, close, not-distant torch.
    (In the early morning the Brothers of Pity
    walked him to the field of Flowers.
    In the early morning they burned him.)

Coda

We map the universe he saw breathe
    alive and peopled by enormous spores—
great fruits of galaxies, each one a seed
    to galaxies that sprout on further shores.

This giant order of huge starry beings
    hurtling their kisses into freezing voids
are not in love with our small human things;
    but he loved them and sought their human laws.

They keep on breeding there in the high heat

atoms that flame to atoms, sun to sun,
and some are victors and some know defeat,
but in the starbuds where the stars come from,

Does any star burn brighter in the flame
than Bruno burning for the human name?

American Voices (1)

Spring raided our street,
broke through the thin glass of daybreak,
found houses asleep,
neighbor's cyclamen bush
redder than it was yesterday.
The Tree of Heaven in our backyard
stretches out a new branch of buds,
certain birds call out their love of trees.
All these objects Spring seized
and said a poet would spell it out.

Spring investigated us this morning:
"Get started!
Get moving
Get on your way!"
Spring held open hearings on the Potomac,
broadcast from the treetops:
"Peace is being born."

Plain Dealer, Cleveland, Ohio:
"I can't help but shudder when the word cobalt no longer describes the shade of blue but conveys the idea of uncontrolled destruction."
—Marion

Winter left us
with thundering casualty lists in our ears
from Iwo Jima and Hiroshima—

and a new love of peace.
May dug us a grave in Laurel, Mississippi.
His last letter:
"They are going to take my life
to keep the Negro down in
the South. Keep on fighting."
—WILLIE MCGEE

Spring investigated our street,
found pavement breaking into daylight,
the Tree of Heaven in our alley
yawning and stretching
and one of us poking for treasure in our trash heaps.

The morning is beautiful, Spring said,
if dogs don't bark at you
and police don't hanker after you
and you sleep the lingering hours into sunlight,
your bed supported by sixteen million Americans.

". . . America's approach to the colonial
races is to treat them as if they were
not human. . . . Now we are reaping what
we have sown. Many in America feel
they are better than Asians; better
than the darker races; better than the
Jews."—*Signed:* MRS. I. W. EPPS
The News Leader, Richmond, Va.

Spring swore out a warrant for breach of peace,
declaring:
This sleeping street is what one sees and smells,
plus a jellied gasoline bomb the street knows
only from a newspaper dispatch:

"Inhabitants asphyxiated in the exact posture
they held when struck, one woman reading her
Sears-Roebuck catalog, in a little hamlet north
of Anyang, the torn page crayoned on mail

order No. 3,811,294: 'a bewitching bedjacket,
coral.' "

Your morning was like this, neighbor,
your naked sleep clothed with the most precious
grammar to spell out how your flesh shines
like a song that sings in your own words:

Courier Journal, Louisville, Kentucky:
"I saw two brothers come home . . . for the
older, war is forever over. As the flag-
draped coffin was taken from the train,
what could the younger boy, who
had escorted his brother 8,000 miles, say to
his parents? What could the President say
if he had been standing there? . . .
–H.D.L.

Between your own letters to the editor, neighbor,
Spring spoke its own plain song:
Soldier, brother, son,
Whose Bunker Hill is this mountain top
you clutched so quietly?
Who owns this blade of grass
you stained with your dying sweat?
How do you spell the name of the village
whose housetops you lifted with your trigger?

The Post, Denver, Colorado:
"Here is the story of a lonely soldier . . .
with a dream of brother love and peace
some day not so far away
from this world of today . . .
P.S. Pray for us out here . . . We need it."
–PFC Ed Gallegos

What recording sings as these letters do
just as they were written,

an epic of the long journey you made
from Indianapolis and Frisco
to land on someone else's island
and kill many strangers,
until you were overpowered by their love of land and
died clutching this strange hill?
Whose sweetheart will plant flowers in your helmet?
Whose mothers will rock their babies to sleep
with lullabies of your coming and going?
Which man's father hails you as liberator?
Who will tell the young warriors
sleeping on the hillsides of Gettysburg
that you loved their hallowed cries?

Seattle Times, Seattle, Washington:
". . . all men are our brothers; a common
doom confronts us all."
—DOROTHY K. SCHMIDT

Brother, soldier, son:
All around you are voices of Spring
everyone can hear singing.

Evening Bulletin, Philadelphia, Pennsylvania:
"I am 12 years old. There is something
puzzling me and I thought maybe you could
help me. If you can, please tell me why
people want to construct such destructive
things as bombs."
—CARYN COLINATI

Now the milkman drives his chariot down our street,
his trumpeting bottles alert our doorsteps
for another day.
The sun pours out on the neighbor's cyclamen bush
a million degrees of exploding atomic heat
and filters through 2,000 million human volts
one more morning of pursuit of liberty and peace . . .

Across the coral isthmus Korea,
    across the human isthmus,
from my own street
    and from the Andean frontier . . .

The Times-Herald, Manitowoc, Wisconsin:
"... The people of America want peace.
Let them have it."
—ARTHUR TRIPPLER

do you hear us?

FROM THE MAYAN BOOK OF CHILAM BALAM

In the beginning there was no sin; we adhered
    to the dictates of reason. There was then
    no sickness, no aching bones, no high fevers,
    no smallpox, no burning chests,
    no abdominal pains, no consumption. We had
    then no headaches; the course of humanity
    was orderly. The foreigners made it
    otherwise when they arrived here.

With the false god, the false word, came the
    beginning of our misery, the beginning
    of strife with purse-snatching, the
    beginning of strife with blowguns,
    the beginning of strife by trampling
    on people, the beginning of robbery
    with violence, the beginning of forced debts.
We were the very poor people who did not
    depart when oppression was put on them.
    It was done by the kinkajous of the
    towns, the foxes of the towns, the
    bloodsucking insects of the towns—
    those who drained the poverty of the
    working people.

But it shall come to pass that tears
shall become the eyes of our jaguar
God. His justice shall descend upon
every part of the earth, straight upon
Ah Kanteria and Ix Pucyola, the
voracious hagglers of the world.

FROM *Land of Roseberries*

AT BEMIDJI FALLS

Neither spirit nor hawk
that was my voice you heard
last night by these willows
calling Wacoba Wacoba

Yes, this is the secret spring
the Indians used to visit.
The woods cover up the sky here.
It is a sound place to make magic.

The waterfall
was there when you were asleep.
Indians used to trap around the bend.
Yes that's the wigwam your ancestor
blew to hell for a dollar and a half.

Neither wind nor wolf
rustled these willows last night
that was my blood you heard
calling Wacoba Wacoba

I free myself by association
I will be Indian,
a native of Kooch. Give me your blood,
give me your copper skin, my fathers.
Get me out of this fix!
Help! I am drowning, Mother,
drowning in the blood
I have spilled
over these waterfalls.

That was no ghost that moved
last night that was my heart you heard
under the willows calling
Wacoba Wacoba

The Execution

And after Governor Faubus led his army against Little Rock and General Walker led his troops against the Supreme Court and Governor Wallace led his bombers against Birmingham
and after 300 years of *if you're white alright, but if you're black, step back*
and after 20 millions of us said *now, right now,* and a quarter million of us marched on Washington
and after the secret army of Governor X and Senator Y bombed the Constitution 41 times in Birmingham and nobody was arrested
we cornered four girl hostages in the basement at Sunday School and executed them using the secret dynamite formula.
And their names were Denice McNair, II, Carrol Robertson, Addie Mae Collins and Cynthia Wesley, all 14.
And Cynthia was identified only by her clothing and a ring.
And they never said a mumbling word, only their memory lies uneasy in us wondering
will we love them as long as the grass shall grow and carry them in our hearts when we shall overcome some day
and really believe they died for us to live?
and the date of the execution was Youth Day at the 16th Street Baptist Church, Birmingham.

"This Nation Under God . . ."

Your agonies
give forth these litle sounds—
such small words
for such deep pain
—Luis Cardoza y Aragón

And God said: Let us make man in our image
with the electric cow prod
burning the genitals
of freedom walkers in Georgia:
with the hidden gun
zeroing Medgar Evers in the back
in Jackson, Mississippi.
And God said: In the beginning was the Word
exploding churches in Birmingham, Alabama
burning up four Sunday School girls.
And God saw everything he had made:
from the poisoned rice fields of South Vietnam
to the student prisoners of Plaquemine, Louisiana
and behold! it was very good:
For the sun cometh with the federal troops in the morning
for those who fight for it.
But what of the city of Baal in Texas.
Will the Oil Worshippers of Dallas
also be saved?
And God said
suffer little children to come unto me.
And when they heard the President was murdered
they shouted *Goody Goody* and clapped their hands.
Eli, Eli—what avenging angel
ordered these televised horrors
to stand the earth still three days
while only our hearts moved?
Will the guilty all be gone to rest

before we suspect
    the bronze idols of General Motors?
    the stone images of Tel and Tel?
    the Gomorrah of Dow Jones averages?
Eli, Eli, must we follow the riderless horse
    to the end of our days?
And the heavens opened and Elijah on a wheel
    said: Behold God has spoken
and the sun cometh in the morning
    for those who help themselves
inherit the freedom of the earth.

from THE SUICIDE

(In memory of a poet who drowned himself)

Regard and guard this skull
whisked among the barnacles
    in a wild lament of moons—
this plain song of a pearl
    that holds the fractures of a world . . .

    From his throat, dreams
sing to ships and sailors
    nightmares of our time:
island universes
    dark with narcotic blooms
vanishing over quicksilver waters.

(O parched! O thirsting! we whispered,
bathe among heather, forget visions
    for long life among turtles.)

So he made the poem
    mountain-climbing with Paul Bunyan;
elsewhere his human yolk
    flowered with anemone

from the crystal of a cancer
that cracks in the shell
for not being born . . .

The chart is the destiny of his year
column for column.
one side for one side,
by the names of the months,
by the number of the suicides.

Not in fall nor winter but in spring
the record grows
the numbers mount
to meet the longer season.

It follows the older years
the days lengthening
the figures rising.

No more for these
nor him,
but numbers
dead to suffering,
immortal in statistics.

Spring is the season
fulfilling the coroner's wisdom,
fattening prophetic numbers
of the older years and older seasons.

Black buds push from the trees,
the rivers bulge, the charts receive
the live numbers
into the lime salts.

The bone spores,
running,
gathered to the rows and columns
from the mountains and the flats,
from the sea-nodules, from the shell ooze,

floating to the sea-bottoms in the waters of the night.
To the marine socket, to the brine pap,
the empty rooms deserted of tortures,
open to sun and to spring
in the waters of the skull,
in the darkness of the numbers.

For the many,
just that remains
of which your Christ is oblivious;
just that escapes
that makes his dream.
So his acts of revelation
are like an ocean in an empty shell,
and his religions
oil in a wound
we are bound to tear open;
          but to fail
allows the moment that discloses
what it is that moves
among the rising to no ends.

Of his aspirations
          what's to be said
but that like our towers
they were sometimes far-reaching

          And this:
he was too much his cousin,
          lay by himself, bred only white mice . . .

There across the Golden Eagle's nest,
his brain struck from its roots
          monstrosities among the vacuums,
cursed, and soaring among the vectors,
among the walkers–
          riders–
               and the heaven-borne.

Creep into the socket, wind,
come down into the skull,
old man of the sea.

Forgive him, sea-petals,
remember him not
(as you will not)
lipped by the wave.
sea-moulded among the conches.

His straw was in the wind
running like an idiot,
with moss in the ears—
devising plans for killing rats,
for evading stenches—
stabbing at the heart
to sustain himself
among the walkers and the riders
and the heaven-borne.

Creep into the sockets,
old man of the sea,
come down into the skull.
Only his song
pounds the Atlantic Highlands,
looking, America, for you.

The Week

Emerson said, "Poems are a form of action." During The Week (which several billion of us thought might be our last), the notes I made for poems weren't designed to spur anybody to action; time seemed to be running out. Leslie Hedley wrote me, "This has been a hell of a week for writing: I feel like a man combing his hair before jumping off a cliff." I answered, "I am trying to finish what I can on the typewriter before it gets incinerated. I have never been fluent in handwriting, especially without a hand."

During The Week, the notes I made for poems had no apparent relation to the real business of No More War. All a poem could do was magnify, like an aerial photograph, the impact of not knowing when you might be saying the last words. What follows, I submit, is evidence of how inconsequential such last words are in the face of the enormity of the fact.

I

Reading about computer war games being played in the Pentagon at the rate of eight hundred million casualties the first hour or two. Also, that our Secretary of Megatons has the highest IQ ever employed in Washington. Maybe it's too high? I wish he were an idiot and would challenge poets of the Warsaw Pact to a series of typewriter confrontations—a kind of escalation just as complex and cheaper. And the result lasts longer, and nobody understands it any better. After the footnotes are collated and the ground zeros are squared and the result is programmed and bing-bangs are scored, no-cities-plus equals the deterrent that can't be stopped.

We are living in the Age of Computer Poems when the real is catching up with the sur-real so fast, all the poem operator has to do is push the first pushbutton, and the poem follows, complete with title:

BUT IS IT ART?

If you have toured the ICBM crematoria
    ahead of time you know
how each has its own guidebook
    with footnotes on how to handle special cases
like accidental blips across the radar screen
    that alert hundred-megaton bombs

to destroy a flock of geese.
SO
I'm killing all birds
to hear how the silence sounds—
not just a few ducks for hunting
but every bluejay, robin, even
fancy birds like egrets
and birds of paradise.
Not war with birds—extinction of birds—
and then, no mistake is possible.
The final mushroom
will be the only bird that sings.

2

Last night I woke up calling out Xmas Island
equations to Lillian but she couldn't
make out what I was shouting because nobody
was left to translate it and it wasn't my
voice—
it was two carrier pigeons conveying battle reports
to Alpha Centauri;
"Everybody was a hero—everybody—particularly
the last two pigeons."

3*

Get drunk and stay drunk to the end;
on what?
wine, words, peace
whatever you choose:
get drunk and stay that way;
then you won't feel the crunch of minutes
on your shoulders.
And if now and then—
on the steps of the White House
on the green edge of a ditch
or in the stone silence of your room—

*Adapted from Charles Baudelaire.

you wake up with a hangover,
insist that the wind, the wave, the star,
    the bird, the clock, or any rocket that flies
    or moves or speaks,
tell you what time it is.
And if the voice on TV, or the star, or the bird
    tell you not to be a pushover for clocks,
stay with it—stay on wine, on poems or peace—
    whatever way you can make it:
only get drunk, stay drunk until the end.

4

How can I keep from singing
when the world sings:
        we have come
    not to destroy but to love,
    to struggle, to live . . .
Look what they did with their land—
turned it into an inexhaustible
wave of peace singing comrade to the world.
You can take a boatride now all over the place—
deserts flowing with milk and roses
canals linking the Seven Seas with wheat and cotton.
Paul Bunyan would have liked this
stepping from the Baltic to the Black Sea
    in hydroelectric boots.
            And who did it?
Men and women like us—
            average height
orbiting carefully into tomorrow
each wave of space singing the future
and the word is
        to live!

5

When the space-trackers in Texas first heard the sound of
    ultrasonic breaths and radar heartbeats from the first

ship in orbit, they asked: "Is it a lion? a monkey? a man?"
But I recognized you, Leonardo.

Not as you died—an exile in a far land—or when you were "also a painter"—in your youth in Florence, or when you were sketching the tortured bodies of horses and men for your lost "Horrors of War,"

rather as you are in your secret notebooks filled with sputnik visions, flying centuries ahead on that batlike wing you hoped to put into orbit yourself.

Forgive us, Leonardo, for having laughed at your stretched-out, bat-wing hands. At last you have arrived beyond the painting and the sculpture and the war machines and waterworks you sold to dukes and kings.

It is your breathing, your heartbeat we hear in the new space-rider spanning the centuries, leaving behind this grave-heavy planet—to join the first man on earth who knew where we were really going.

6

Just when I needed a little diversion like Charlie Parker, the only station I could get was Conelrad and a lugubrious voice saying:

"Get under your bed and play dead,
and then crawl, don't walk, to the
nearest ashtray."

7

Bernard Shaw had just said: "Only on paper has humanity yet achieved glory, beauty, truth, knowledge, abiding love," when suddenly all the paper in the world went up in flames.

8

Earth fault
slipped
uncontrolled.

Algae
    began
where stone had been.
    The constellations
unamazed
    no provision
to undo the done
    establish the norm.
Silent
    sullen
spore in the rocks
    multiplying and dividing
leaving our vast
    fossil impact tagged:
"Last of placentals
    descended from
fish eggs and TV screens
    plus
pulse code modulations
    kissing and killing
during the commercials
    and looking for the rent."

9

(Just before the kitchen boils over)

Faces gleam through the kitchen window where the
        traffic light from the corner
blinks its eye at the rain like Ezekiel on the wheel.
There are trees in the Himalayas bare like bunches
            of black violets
and the dark clusters will soon be white with snow
    that hangs unfallen in the mist above the mountains of
    Tibet.
The milk I heat in the aluminum pot on the stove is a
    music with molecules oscillating over the flame until they
    lift their peacock spray in the white orgasm of the boil
singing like a psalmist: the milk is my shepherd . . .

10

Some poets take peyote for visions; all I do is read the newspapers. One recurrent nightmare is an impossible leap across a billion overkills to tomorrow's zeros. When I come to my senses we are all still here, but I have a hangover in terms of the language problem.

On a scale of recorded talk, our oldest hieroglyphics date about 10,000 B.C. And now we face a geological catastrophe in which not only all people but all written words will be obliterated.

I dream of a space ship encircling the earth, timed to re-enter in a thousand years with a cargo of Homer, Tu Fu, Dante *et al*, to tell any strangers who wonder about what was going on here back in the Overkill Era.

For we live in the age of "controlled response" when we all eat and work and love as if we would each live out our three-score-ten with whatever personal destiny we have. That's crazy! There's a man on the hotline going round taking names. And he isn't Mozart or Einstein or Socrates. Yes, I'm sentimental about that. If the human race is going to join the ruins of the dinosaurs ahead of time, I'd like to think this was being done at least by Schopenhauer who suggested a quick finish might be its best tomorrow.

But we live on the whims of men in custom-tailored suits, who ride in black limousines, and whose addition to human insight and knowledge would hardly challenge Billy the Kid.

To be murdered by idiots! Not in a dark alley but by a web of fossil thought that has a claw on the pushbutton to disaster!

It's against that prospect that all our poems are nihil compared to the human presence in the IBM Age when no one knows which "limited bombing" will lead to another, and so on, *ad infinitum.*

And now the Moses and St. Peter of our final judgment is speaking on TV about the "free world." And I'm sneaking in this little prayer, begging him to keep on talking. Even if it's not a poem, I have a special love for the rasp of his voice. As long as I can hear him drawl it out I know there's another instant of hope for our syllables (and our country) to last one more beautiful breath, when we were all here talking together really.

II

(A final word) about the children. I have lately come to the notion that for sheer beauty you can have Michelangelo, Brancusi, the Taj Mahal and the Greek temples at Paestum. I vote for the children, particularly around the age of five. Infants are monkey faces to me. And about nine they become premature adults. In between, about four to seven, is the best thing the human race has done. I have collected poems from them that I want to publish some day—if we last long enough. Meanwhile, let me close this gasp with a poem I just got from Laura, a five-year-old beauty with Titian hair:

A person is like a clock
When the hands don't move any more
and it doesn't tick-tack any more
then you are dead.
But the clock is just broken.

Letter to the President

Poets, said Shelley, are the unacknowledged legislators of the world. Often we recognize in what they say our own inarticulate feelings and thoughts. Today we are presenting a poet's letter to the President of the United States . . .

During the next few moments you will hear parts of the letter as he writes it, alternating with poems that are forming in his mind. He has just read a passage from the late Polish poet Julian Tuwim: "It is becoming more difficult to speak and more painful to keep silent."

And, as the poet tries to find words for his letter to the President, this Spring Song *runs through his mind:*

What weather of shelters–
our own or anybody's analogs–
feeds down the icecaps into the computers
its song of fallout
this spring?
What crawl of cobalt
cracks the blood count with bells,
dissolves the crystals
and divides the lovebirds in the laboratories
from the dead?

Grasses that hold footprints of ants,
neutrons where the ladybugs go,
all the jets –missiles– milk and roses,
swing an orbit of rockets
the human ear echoes when it hears
in any isotope
or lover's touch
the song of megatons
this spring.

Dear Mr. President:
What's at stake for me is the survival of my country –not as a geological crater, but as a pure independent nation. Naturally this is a big love affair for my life because I have no other place like home.

At the end of the rainbow
is a boy and a girl
In every language it is the same.
Why envy Assyrians their roses?
or begrudge mothers of Oaxaca
their olives?
The gates of heaven are waiting to be opened up

in Topeka, Kansas.
Why not love each other at home
and leave the girls of the islands
to other swimmers?

It's not the idea of being turned into cinders, along with Lillian and our little cottage in the South Jersey pine barrens; at 65 I don't have that life expectancy that makes such an ultimate difference. What bothers me is the shame of it; that I should be responsible in what I haven't done or done enough to keep my country from becoming a sandlot where the pueblo civilization of the Manhattan Islanders used to flourish.

O outriggers of the Pacific
believe my shame, my tears:
for too many terms
there has been no office in the Capitol
for the Collector of Poetry.
The Summit hears only songs to his praise.
But those who are wisely governed,
do they need porches
covered with edicts?
schools doors closed to decent children?
The true voice of the people
the Collector of Poetry should collect
and the criticized should take heed in time:
Soldier–stay beautiful as you are
AT HOME!

It doesn't cheer me up that other gardens won't be pretty sights either, and I am not worried about the future of the human race –they will survive– along with interesting people from Tibet, Tierra del Fuego and the Yukon– as socialist descendants of the lemurs and dinosaurs. The amoeba in us will not be forgotten.

Among 5-star beetles in military postures
polaris whirligigs and other master ghouls
all workers in putrefaction
programming our maximum survival.

And from a recent book entitled, "How to Save A Million Lives," I quote: "The Pure-City Strategy, originally identified with the Navy has fallen from grace. The Cities-Plus doctrine has grown. Devastation and No-City are both Counter-Force, but Devastation is called Spasm War and No-City is called Central War. Both Pure City and Cities-Plus are termed Finite Deterrence by the Air. Admirals have dropped finite, the word has lost precise meaning. They prefer to call their theory Stable Deterrence or Mutual Deterrence. Various writers have tried to straighten out the terminology but their efforts have not caught on." (Unquote)

But wait!
Have you tried a poem?
If not
the electronic dictionaries will curse you.
The syntax cyclotron will melt your bones
and you will not be heard looking for credibility
among minutemen, Honest Johns and other
ghosts of words
that used to ring the registers so sweetly
between the Golden Gate and Hatteras.

I suppose it's my bourgeois upbringing—this persistence of nationalism in me—but it's the fate of my own country that bothers me most.

Humanity entire can take care of itself—that's its business, and it appears well trained to the job—having already come through the fall of Egypt, Greece, Rome, the Tang Dynasty and Charlemagne the Great. But my poor little United States—so fragile in its 200-year-old polished surface, so disassociated even now, with 20 million of us insisting "let's unite the United States!"

The sun climbs the sun ladder;
he comes from his hiding place
with pollen in his hands
for all the children
to inhale the sacred breath of life
their own way,
Africa! Africa!
The sun cannot rise alone.
You say you wait the dawn?
You are the dawn!
Across the heat barrier
the golden life flames with certainties
Across the Congo and the Mississippi
your children assemble their multitudes,
each a sun lighting up a new world.

What will become of Abe Lincoln in his Washington Memorial if they kill him again and this time for good? Who will be as proud as Whitman was of the young men who lie in the battlefields of Gettysburg? And where, in all that's left of the world's geography, will there ever be a race like us again?

And here's a Venezuelan poet's warning for Abraham Lincoln:

Captain, I am looking for you,
for I've heard they're out to murder you again—
and this time we know it.
Listen to the footfalls
of those who are plotting to let locusts
roam over you.
And already are gloating at the green feast ahead.
Watch out, Captain, watch out!

The wheat stalks are trembling and the sky darkens—
their pincers and mandibles threaten you—watch out!
There, in your box in the theatre—
I know it, and I tell you:
An eclipse is falling over the most beautiful fields.
Not a stone will remain on stone
and your city is already weeping.
If they kill you again,
who will draw the honey from you?
who will draw from you
the milk of human peace?
If they kill you again,
who will look after you?
If they kill you again,
it will not be possible any more—
not even in the wild laurel of dreams—
for the hills above your grave
to flower again, day and night.
Captain, I am looking for you
to tell you they're after you
with the bead of their guns—
to shoot you again, to open up a new wound,
to kill you with new bloodless death,
where nothing could grow
and the hills above you would perish.
And then, where
would we be able to bury you,
those of us who follow your voice
and drink deep from your sad eyes—
where,
if you were not living—but dead?

From Naples and France and the Netherlands and all the islands we came to kill our Indians and make their fertile lands our own, and then to die because our neighbors couldn't be snuffed out like the Cherokees.

And we hear the voice of Patrice Lumumba—

I am dead, dead, dead!
They cut out my heart in Stanleyville.
They left my lungs in Leopoldville.
My eyes they gouged out in the mines of Katanga.
And they blew my brains to bits in Kasai.
They have taken my rivers, my mountains, my jungle,
I have nothing left but the fragments of myself
that come together in you, my brothers,
in the four corners of the world.

I am confessing my own weakness—it's not all humanity that's at stake for me, but the idea of what we in the United States could have been.

For what other people could have made socialism such a sport so quickly as the boys and girls of Harlem, Chicago's South Side, the cliffdwellers of the Golden Gate and points north and south? It's not our obliteration as concrete physical substance that's my main gripe—it's the idea of us now—that if we go out we go out as a lie.

. . . and Horace said it to the Roman people 2,000 years ago . . .

Where are you rushing to
in those uniforms you just
got from the cleaners?
Haven't you left enough soldiers
in the Pyrenees and Gaul?
Are you disturbed that one of us
won't burn the Scythian towers
or parade through the streets of Carthage;
or that, according to the Delphic Oracle,
your flame-throwers might get scorched with their own
fire?

Why not try wrestling
grizzly bears on the Appian Way?
Or twist the dragons of Cathay here at home?
Answer me—are you full of Sicilian wine,
the way you are hot-footing it to hell?
Or are you just snowblind from crossing
the Alps too often?

It's our entire future, as it exists, this instant, for if tomorrow isn't already a glowing daybreak just about to come over the horizon, we are already dead—and more than dead—the wild geese will make their arctic orbit over the Atlantic shore and never know what great ballplayers and mechanics and dancers used to live in Hoboken and San Antonio.

I am sorry for all the snowbirds and spiders and squirrels that used to love us because we left such beautiful crumbs before Times Square became a toothless skull.

I am sorry for all the hopes that Thomas Jefferson dreamed of and Nat Turner died for. And all the lovers who hid in parks and dived into the sand at Jones Beach will not save us from not even becoming a might-have-been.

But at the last moment of desperation
a gravity experiment saves you.
The primary frequency standard
maintains atomic time
also
Ephemeris time
defined in terms of
the square root of minus-one.
You see how useful atomichron seconds have become?
A way is opened to a merry
And controlled
Christmas (Island)
basic to America's Posture.

PROVIDED
it turns out to be just a communications difficulty in the early warning system. "Meanwhile General Power has ordered 400 nuclear-armed bombers into readiness" because the wrong bulb flickered.

AND I
am already exploring the ways to make paper survive (not wondering, as Shakespeare did, why calamity should be full of words) but hammering out an elegy for all the children of our Inter-glacial Age.

We will go out not like a light but like a black death . . . the rest of the world wouldn't let our rats spread. It's our absence from all the holidays and festivals and dances of tomorrow that is breaking my back today. For the only death is to die alone.

This is the time of the limited suicide when I keep you from killing yourself with machine guns and bayonets,
because I have a 100-megaton bomb produced by the Snake God who doesn't care how you get there—or in how many installments—
as long as the national debt passes away in time for another generation of shock troops to renew the charge.
It then becomes essential to know precisely how crazy the other computer is getting to be
if you want to keep the edge of deterrence open at your end.
Also, at what microsecond of the day he reaches his median, so you can adjust your early dew warning system to his ups and downs,
Under these circumstances, our neighbors lived a purely normal life,
the birthrate increased, the death rate declined,

the 9 percent unemployment got built in for life,
and everybody lived happily in the suburbs of forever after.

Across the human isthmus, where the ultimate deterrent awaits the final posture, and our North American dream is still alive, I am begging for that one word from all of us that will make our beautiful tomorrow alive today.

And as our Amerindian ancestors put it:

What is more beautiful
than the land that has no grave
because there is no fear,
Where bravery doesn't bleed
because there is no enemy,
where the warriors of the Hundred and One Nations
uproot the tallest pine tree
and in the hole that's left
drop their bombs and guns,
deep in the underearth,
throw all their weapons,
and plant again the tree. Then
when the Great Peace is won
we will find the land
where truth is without a name
because there is no lie;
where charity has no home
because there is no hunger;
where nobody is an Unknown
Hero any more,
and no one is a seer—
because the light of wisdom
is everywhere . . .

and love
LOVE

L O V E
(also more love)
dividing the sun
putting ribbons on the storms
turning each body into a flower
looking, America, for you.

American Voices (2)

Across Jersey sand barrens
night is cradled in the arms of pine branches,
peach blossoms are shaking on the bough.
A jet plane from Pomona Air Base
zips its star across our sky,
but the ground of liberty is still gained by inches.

My name is Larry. My letter appeared in the
Wayne University Collegian, Detroit, Michigan:
"The world is not Americo-centric, and we are
participants in a world community, not masters
of it."

In South Jersey
across the Land of Lenapes
the deer trail is hidden in the cedar swamps,
cranberry pippins edge out of their moss.
In Bridgeton
a wife longs by her window:

Your ring warms my finger but you
have gone to the neighborhood of death.
I am washing the powder from my face
the lipstick from my lips.
When can we both lean by the wind-blown curtains
and see the tears dry on each other's face?

In South Jersey
the wild laurel breathes over our tomato patches.
A pine wind dusts our hands and faces—
a farmer turns in his sleep wondering—
will morning bring radium or rain?

In a room in Vineland
a mother is parting from her son.
She cries but no sound breaks from her voice.
She clutches at him though her arms are still.
Who hears her song:

On the gray birches the moon shines cold.
Soon it will be warm in the woods of South Jersey.
When will my son return?
He was always a man of peace
and played baseball in the spring.

In South Jersey
whippoorwill calls sharpen our ears,
blueberry bushes wave through the dark
and peach blossoms send out perfume
to make a peace treaty with spring.

In South Jersey
the sun is marching north
15 miles a day.
The tips of our scrub oaks are separating
into pink threads. Swamp magnolias
are crackling with light.
In Mays Landing
a girl reads her sweetheart's letter . . .

March, march, march
separated by 10,000 miles,
each in our corner.
The road is so far,
When shall we meet?

What is left us
but wanting to be together?
A copper coin or a stone
outlives any of us.
Only a good name endures.
We are all brothers,
each a branch from the same tree . . .
If I live I shall return,
if I do not,

we shall live in each other
forever.

I am Margaret. My letter was in the Free Press, Detroit, Michigan.

"I will shortly become a mother for the first time, and this more than any single factor dramatizes to me the need for world peace."

In South Jersey
we do not yearn for the cedars of Lebanon.
At dawn we drink the alarm-clock blues.
At dusk we eat the petals from our days.
We grieve over endless hungry children.
We mark down carefully how much we can endure.
We grind the tractor on the side of the sun,
flick the sky's face with an oakleaf,
order the bridgekeeper at Somers Point—
OPEN UP!

Over Brigantine we look at the sky.
The rainbow we planted has arrived.
Our sunlight is already
bending across the mountain of today.
We are here!

FROM *Translations from Scorpius*

Signing In:

I'm signing in from Eta Carinae, the nebula from which
the earth sprang.
I'm surrounding myself with African masks, atomic
orbits, scrolls of the Torah, Aztec sun dials and
The New York Times
And I can hear our Venus probe report from outer space:

At the edge of the loop
that holds it all together,
the string is frayed . . .
no square root of minus one,
no second law of entropy,
just a small frayed string
trying to tell us while it can:
Man, I'm not that strong myself.

MY SPECTRUM ANALYSIS

(*"The detector recorded an outstanding X-ray source in the constellation of Scorpius."*
—Scientific American)

I

We are the should-be's of collapsed
supernovae

doomed to winter it among galactic halos
in the cool universe of undisturbed suns.
There is no pain
only
a swift wind of hydrogen
sweeps us
through centuries of magnetic storms
to an immolation we do not know.
We are the diffuse gas of electronic
degeneracy
cast in cosmic particles in the flesh
and in the low density of your make-
believe
we kiss your mirror image
goodbye, so long, it's been good to
know you
in the full spectrum of celestial radiation.

2

It took me six billion years
to get just that distance from the sun
I need to breathe
and just near enough our oxygen supply
to stay alive.
And now some people want to send me back
to the hydrogen I left behind.
Can't the Keeper of the Computers realize
I finished my share
of the glowing gas phase
when Father Alijera first lit his campfire
with stars
20 billion degrees Centigrade ago?

3

Last night I rocketed
above the radio region of the spectrum.

No ligaments there of our twisted selves
so fouled up
nobody suspects anyone
of telling the truth,
we were all lovers in celestial bodies.
And there I saw you,
childbrother,
in the womb of the galactic center
aching to be born
one minute ahead of the appointed
birthday full of singing telegrams
and flowers arriving just in time
to say we too can love
and live
above the Geiger-counter level.

4

For the first three billion years of inter-
galactic dog eat dog
not a spiral nebula laughed. Followed an
additional three billion years of cosmic
alienation.
Not one microwave in the Crab Nebula
cracked a smile.
Finally one bright green morning a mutation
called Archimedes
joked about changing the world with a lever.
And a one-minute routine
of scientific vaudeville began called The
World as Good Fun.
But the real gasser came the next minute
when some Pentagonian computer
thought it was the spiral nebula in
Andromeda attacking us.
And the last smile of the last child went
into orbit and cried silently forever after.

5

Guerrilla Girl!
The peach blossoms are redder because rain fell
overnight where you fell.
The free people of earth weep with joy remembering
the gift of your body.
Was your husband gone? Did you refuse to talk?
Did they open up your womb and take out the child?
Guerrilla Girl! The cold mountain turns dark green
in the morning sun
where your dreams are a blue sky rolling among the
purple hills.
Though the head be severed from the body the heart
never changes.

6

Meanwhile
there are enough megatons in the world
to kill everybody 12 times . . .
and the faintly disappearing edges
dissolve behind the oakleaf
where the shell on the beach bends
and the lie disappears just around the
corner drug store
where the credibility of our oyster beds
will not save us
from the 12th death.

7

At the last moment
I learned to believe in failure
but only on a galactic scale
of burned-out supernovae.
Elsewhere,

among the carbon compounds
where our love affair goes on,
the sweet kiss of dialectics
keeps whispering:

What's really happening
is terribly superior
to any history
any story, any divinity
any super-reality
and even the spectrum analysis
is moving toward the red.

In the Library Stacks

Dear Pony-Tail:
Don't stare at the 42 hairs on my head
as if I were the ghost of Confucius.
I, too, am researching here
for that dustless row
of mint-fresh volumes
that gives all the answers.
Have you tried
the Cro-Magnon library
downstairs
just one floor
above the Pleistocene deposits?

Dante's 700th Anniversary

L'amor che move il sole e l'altre Stelle

I know everybody does it—
elephants, goldfish,

petunias, too—
    but to love
(every day!)
    our screaming spiral
nebula and all its
    drunken brother galaxies—
(even the finks and sell-out
    constellations that
roll you for a drink
    and then burn up)—
that's the inter-stellar kiss
    (I guess)
that lights the sun
    and other lonesome stars
        like people.

Message from Bert Brecht

And don't think
    art
is that actor over there
    talking
to that other one
    upstage.
He's
    the third one
you don't see
    talking
to that other one
    you can't hear
offstage.

I Belong

There are three billion billion billion constellations
(the sky book says) but I am a patriot of the
Milky Way. It gives me a thrill when I look
out the telescope at *our* galaxy. I mean–I
know where I belong–just like those two titmice feeding together outside my window, and
right now flying off together–I, too, know
I have a home, an identity established not
only by national boundaries, common speech,
etc., not just by our own beautiful sun, and
its planets, moons, asteroids, but by our own
dear galaxy. O lover
in your pure feathery light, across thousands of billions
of spiral nebulas, you are the best of all
galaxies
and I know you love me too, for out of the vast riches
of your fiery interstellar sperm you have
given me inalienable rights to life, liberty
and the pursuit of happiness
and my own little life to cool.

Epitaphs

Epitaph for the Sidereal Equator

Giving birth to Yes
    just once won't do. You
have to keep at it every
    day. The instant you
doubt, the seams begin
    to fall apart and the holes
start dropping to
    the sidereal bottom
where the giant star spider
    broods in darkness
alone.

Epitaph for My Punctuation

Not the absurd, not the inconsequential,
    just the comma of being here
        among milk bottles & constellations
in love with our parenthesis of passage
    between Andromeda and Peekskill
where the world's apostrophes collapse
    into the oneness of all ditto marks & galaxies
        including lovers doing the hyphen
along the mountain-folding
    question mark of Palisades Parkway.

For A. J. Muste

(Adapted from Petrarch, Canzione 128)

Today (he said) gives us always
new reasons to live in others
even those with birdseed for hearts,
who don't want to live
and don't know how to love.
Nothing can keep them too from arriving
when the sky opens
and the sun lands
full of tomorrow's peace
everyone is waiting to kiss
after their napalmed yesterdays.
Meanwhile (he said)
with our deeds we are waking you
asking you don't stay asleep:
don't turn your back on the truth:
listen to us: hear us:
how can we stop being afraid?
Out of my heart I'm telling you
calling on you
pleading with you
hear us: O peace
peace
peace.

Your Centennial Is My Centennial

Poets of the world unite and celebrate
your centennial with mine.
It's true I was born in 1897

and you were born even later
but in the century of the H-bomb
can you wait a hundred years
to find out if you'll be here?
P.S.
Please respond by return poem, letter, or kisses.
Everything will be printed (including kissmarks).
In the vast centennial of the poets who can't be stopped
COLLECTORS & ANTIQUARIANS
PLEASE NOTE:
The first printing of this poetry explosion
is limited to 14 billion copies
printed on diamond paper to insure
our century will survive Carbon 14
Strontium 90
civilian shelters
and other incinerators of the human touch.

R. I. P.

(*after François Villon*)

Walter died suddenly at 3 A.M.
of an insufficiency of arterial beats
he never bothered writing a poem about.
We often see his kind around the Movement
swinging between being everything to all people
and a stick of gum to his grandchildren.
Just before he shoved off he wrote us his
epitaph:

After you have burned the remains
and gotten rid of the ashes—
(the cheapest way—no
little urn in the Chapel!)—

if you have a moment between drinks and paying bills
    shake your pen over the table
        or on the floor for me—
a tiny drop of ink
    tomorrow's children
        will wipe off easily.

3

The Autobiography of My Poems

To Martha Millet (A poet and an old friend), January 29, 1959:

I don't quite agree with practically everybody. That's what drives me to poems.

The poem can indicate the circles within which it ripples. I mean there is a larger circle (didn't Emerson say it?) which the poem indicates by nods, gestures, rhythms, nudges, skipped beats and all.

In prose you have to SPELL IT OUT. I am against prose even while writing it.

It's not enough to be against kings, tyrants, feudal rulers, *et al.* It is necessary also to be against that policeman, the universe. Poets are bound to turn their typewriters against geological despots.

Then you can fly and be an Ignou. Who is Ignou? I want

to get to a question we can't discuss in prose. I affirm Ignou, but only at the last gasp of the jet stream.

O, I can make sense too but I will never get elected on that platform.

You will learn nothing from this. And that is my aim. An occasional illumination, a once-a-year star rocket that burns its pinwheels so we will all know there is flame going on.

To Angela (my youngest daughter) February 12, 1959:

The real situation, I think, is that the real situation is much more complicated than I can begin to deal with, except as it begins to turn into a poem—sometimes not a successful evolution. I mean the poem may not come out of the situation at all—just a dermoid cyst of a poem—a hank of words with hair on it.

So I am learning to try and keep my mouth shut unless I can spell it out to make sense in the only way I can.

When I started—or, rather, resumed writing poems (1953) —one thing I had in mind (and said, also) was: Nobody pays me any mind when I try to beat it into them with prose; maybe if I begin to write poems again, people will pay some attention to what I am trying to get done.

The outcome has been different. It only has meant that people pay no attention to me now except as it is a poem.

I am doomed not to be taken seriously.

Nobody believes anything I am driving at because—O, Walter, he is a poet!

I can't go back now—it's too late. I have reached the point of no more return; my only aim is to avoid delusions.

Poems have never been a literary pursuit for me but a way of life. When I was working for the *Worker,* that also was a way of life—I put everything in it. It was my poem for that period.

Now I feel that poems are the extension of journalism by other means.

I don't have any other life than the one I am trying to express as I fulfill it, and vice versa.

So I am not a person aside from the *Worker* when I edit it, or the poems when I edit the poems.

I realize that is a crazy way to live.

So I don't blast about it. I try to keep it secret.

The struggle to achieve a society in which people live poems does not take place in the abstract. It is a struggle around concrete poems by real people—maybe Isaac Rosenberg, the English war poet; maybe Walter, the USA peace poet, etc. I do pretty much the same for others as I have been done for by others.

It is puzzling at times to find your Paris work of 1930 being printed and read and making, or beginning to make, a dent in 1960. So I do arrive at the wisdom that the main point is to survive.

We all, one way or another, have this problem. The artist's problem is not unique. He simply shows on his skin the cicatrice everybody else hides.

Nobody can fail you in this adventure. It is people who fail themselves—their possibilities unfulfilled.

I love children for their present. At seven, something happens to the non-survivors. This is a statistical certainty.

So I write elegies for statistics.

I really don't want to be understood.

Glenwess Acott can be understood.

My game is a rug-pulling act.

The other reality you suspect but don't dare acknowledge.

I have gone far past ordinary politics. I am in the age of surrealist politics.

And when we all get there, there will be singing such as you never dreamed.

I may not be heard there, but I will dream.

To François Hugot (young French critic and poet, and a translator of my poems), June 8, 1960:

I used to say (1929): Not poems as literature but as a bridge over the desert of our age.

All my work has this signature: It is not a direct picture

but an underwater angle—out of the corrupt sickness of our time into the possibilities of making a poem; it is a sign of our time's decline, as well as a pointer to how we can create out of any situation—provided we know what time it is, and which way the clock is moving.

To create out of death remains the artist's hope in the United States. We may be making a Byzantine kind of art that will not happen again.

When millions of people paint pictures and write poems, and the division of labor is eradicated so that millions are artists, we may not get that tension between extremes that dominates the work of Eluard or Picasso. It will be a new poem we will be looking for. . . .

At best we are reporters, recording how it is—in biography rather than poetry. This helps to account for the verbal texture, the use of ordinary words, scientific lingo. To avoid "poesy"—to see ordinary people and ordinary language as the creative stuff of our age.

Mary Austin wrote, years ago, that there was a connection between soil and language rhythms. That's why only the United States has produced the rhythms of our Indian poems or of Whitman, i.e., the native style. I think the soil—if seen in a geologically social way—accounts for what we are doing with language today and with forms.

The artist's job is to reveal the instantaneous present. I have tried to report human experience at my particular instant within the country I inhabit, but with the consciousness of the rest of the world. I call this "socialist surrealism"; but I don't ask you to accept my definition or to use my terminology.

Montesquieu said that good writing is the art of omitting transitional thought. In poems, it is the adventure of "words in arrested time." The artist is a master of revelations, adept at reading the entrails of beasts; he visits the oracle at Delphi; he has to be able to join the Hopi snake dancers . . . the dragon dancers of China. No one of the mysteries can be penetrated today with the politics of yesterday.

It is in this sense that Rimbaud has to be understood today: "It is absolutely necessary to be modern." Some interpret this thought as an injunction to describe social decay; they think the next piece of dirt and the next is the last word. Society can always get worse; there is no hope in society as society. Our only hope as human beings is to transform society into its opposite.

We cannot imagine the people of tomorrow. If we could, we would be like them. All we know is that without them we all die today. It is this tiny glimpse of the future without which today is unbearable. That is what Leonardo told us long before Marx worked it out in scientific terms; Aeschylus and Aristophanes have been saying it through the centuries: The artist is the first politician. That, naturally, is the way the whole story starts—not once, but over and over again. "In the beginning, there was the word." All we have to do is to record the facts, arrange them so they make sense. . . . I used to call it (1930) "The World as Poem." But that sounded pompous, so now I sometimes call it "Reality Prime."

P.S. There is an underground movement that keeps alive the biography of the earth. Our kind of poems are not likely to happen again. It is the instantaneousness of our lives that some of us are trying to catch. For years, while I was silent, and often after I resumed writing, I thought: It is necessary to write the poem of tomorrow today; I even had a title: Tomorrow is Today. But that approach would produce slogans, posters—not art.

My definition of a poet: "a re-write man." Of poems: "The continuation of journalism by other means." At the decisive moment, you have to be verbally equipped to act.

We expect from the poet only the last word that everybody misses because it is about to fade out. For it is not only the poet's role to reveal—he always holds back the final word; he appears to be saying something, but he is silent in the face of what he really sees . . . or spells it out so simply nobody believes him.

Simplicity may also have a false face. The Medicine Man. The Indian Mask. The dancers in the rites of Dionysus. The Totem Pole. We have a long story to tell: the Dyaks knew it and the Eskimos know it—only in the igloos of Manhattan the story breaks into glass everybody thinks he can see through.

Of course, we transcend literature. And no one can ever tell when or where it will happen. I get it from a 20-year-old poet in Jamaica nobody knows; or César Vallejo in Peru; it is heard in the last words of the Haymarket martyrs ("let the voice of the people be heard"), or in Vanzetti's speech to the court ("this agony, our triumph . . ."), or Bruno at the stake. When the fire burns in the poet, it melts everything into a new creation.

We are adventurers on Ezekiel's wheel—extending the spokes of our words into space and always returning to the hub. As you know, I am saying in another way: The rites of Dionysus, the burning of the old god. Out of it comes the "Drinking Gourd" and other Negro songs; Chu Yuan giving out his "Poem of Everlasting Sorrows" before he jumped into the waters. The minimum demand of creation: that something be given up, some of life be sacrificed, some of it done away with so that something new arrives.

Thus, the "anti-poem." To kill the dying verse of yesterday's elegy for the simultaneous birth of today's song. Of course, today's song doesn't seem to sing; only yesterday's, to which we are accustomed. Everybody knows *Leaves of Grass* reached one reader its first year—Emerson. That's the pure mechanics of the creative act and makes abolutely no difference. Nobody is interested in what the poet or poem goes through. All that is of interest is the arrival.

To Howard McCord:

About the poetry-politics love affair in my life (you asked): From my first anonymous book (1925) my work has had two poles: Intensely personal; intensely social.

Personal: not only in the love poems but also in the "letters" to people like Cubby ("To an Unsuccessful Suicide") etc. "Every poem is a love poem"; this applies also to the best of the letters (as in *Imaginary Daughter*, *Loving You in the Fallout*). In fact, my work seems to be culminating in "letters" rather than verse. In quotes because I don't make that division between poems and verse, letters and poems. It's just a different way of spelling out the poem that's going on all the time.

The point I am trying to clarify is that there is no barrier between art and politics. Art is a transformation of experience. We are all political zoons. But very few of us transcend our politics and write:

> Give me my scallop-shell of quiet
> My staff of faith to walk upon,
> My scrip of joy, immortal diet,
> My bottle of salvation, etc.

And yet Raleigh was so political he had his head chopped off because of it.

The issue is the poem of it, not the politics of it. It's the act of being alive that I see as a poem—as Calvin Hernton does, or Ishmael Reed. Every little now and then we catch it on the typewriter. And it is that transmission that we need so badly in the United States. The poem has become the last ceremonial, the final act of the Rain Dancers, the communion between you and the good earth. And so it's natural that my final pages these days are geologic and galactic. We touch the universe or we die. . . .

What I tried to do was make a poem out of making a poem. So the non-poem, even the silence of the ink, became part of the scream. But so carefully organized all you heard was the kiss.

My humanity, communicability, audience-relation, etc. are part of the mystic maze I have wound around myself. My aim is to lose you, to leave you searching for what has disappeared. I am baffled as you are. And this, I think, is what we have in common-our bewilderment. The key to mine is everybody's confusion, so organized it seems to be clarity.

I think one thing that helped is that to my very last book I was always an outsider. It's not only what I did, but what I wanted to do and tried to (that is, my goal), that was completely out of the literary perspective. The critic who adjusted his literary lens at my work wouldn't get me into focus at all. I'm not even trying to do what he is looking for. We have different ideas as well as ideals.

In my work the juxtaposition of ideas and scientific adventures of words take the place of sex description in other books. I am the ideological counterpoint of the writer whose work is often banned by the censor as "pornographic." Perhaps the unforgiveable sin was that I saw the common experience of our time as a poem.

Thus the key to my long period of unacceptability was not the use of four-letter words everyone uses in conversation to denote beautiful natural functions and organs, but how I was also in love (when the sewage truck went lumbering past) with "loud garbage."

This love affair with ordinary things culminated in my approach to social revolution as another "rites of spring," with working people carrying through the ritual burial of the old god and the birth of the new. What can be dirtier in the eyes of the established order than that?

To Joe North, October 25, 1965:

Poems (or any other art) relate to the question: What time is it?

If this is hard to grasp today, consider another time—the age of Homer, for example. Where do you turn but to Homer? Or to Shakespeare and Marlowe for the Elizabethan Age; Michelangelo and Leonardo for the 16th-century renaissance?

Each artist gives you more than his age, but it is only

through the particular verbal texture of his age that he transcends its limitations and shows you the clock that never stops.

Thus, the poet's art of words—not as evasion of reality but as its oral revelation: It exists and can be lived.

As soon as we read the way Whitman says it: "I contain multitudes," or Calvin Hernton, "There'll be no jitterbugging in the streets this Fourth of July," we recognize we knew these things before—only it took the man from Brooklyn or Harlem to make it explicit, say the unsayable in the lingo of his time.

Yes, you can see eternal things in a grain of sand with Blake. But few of his contemporaries did. The point I am making is the relevance of seeing that grain of sand today, in today's poem. Because it's not quite the same grain of sand—it just looks like it. If you doubt me, test the difference in the rhythms and language of each decade. Go back a second or two (on the geologic time scale) and you arrive at Chaucer, for whose English you need a glossary.

All this relates to your proposal—that we run stuff about me in *Dialog*. The moment you mention the word "poem" or "poet," we are in danger of losing readers; many are likely to move on to something they can use, something they think relates to their lives in our time—like a discussion of existentialism or The Movement.

The essential framework around us is always in danger of escaping our grasp because it exists in the next degree of vision. It's that degree the poet spells out for us now, today. So when you say: "So-and-so has expressed for us the essence of our atomic age," that doesn't mean a thing to most people—it's a blurb. They can get along without it unless you, as critic, convince them they need it if they want to be totally alive to our time.

We are in a constant search for creativity; in a day-by-day struggle for *our* brand of it; it is always slipping away from those who boast of it to those who fight for it.

All our emotions are different in the 1960's because of

what happened in Hiroshima in the 1940's. . . . Spring, love, children—you name it—the words are no longer the same with Strontium 90 in the air. This is the inescapable framework for all our lives, all our poems. Not that every poem is a poem about peace and war; on the contrary, "every poem is a love poem." What differs is the essential framework that surrounds the poem—as it does our lives.

Consider an example that lies close to hand—these lines from my *American Voices*: "Spring raided our street . . . / Spring investigated us this morning . . . / Spring swore out a warrant for a breach of the peace. . . ." This poem takes place within the context of the kind of lines that could have been written only in a period when anybody who was anybody was being investigated. And yet, that poem is not about investigations at all. It is an elegy for a soldier who died in Korea.

Does it matter? Does it make any difference? Not to the President, not to the Secretary of War. All the poem can do is to give us a momentary dilation of our vision. Once you get that wider angle, other things will also relate differently —not all the time perhaps, but in those moments when you are alive and most aware of being alive.

So, people write love poems not at the moment of kissing, but later, to get into words that endure the instant touch that is otherwise gone so rapidly.

None of this will by itself save the world and all our kisses from being blown to hell. What we are talking about is the enormous value of that instant of being alive that the poem spells out for us, and thus in its way helps us to fight for life whenever and wherever we can. Remembering that not to know and love the tragedy of your own life is not to know the joy of being here at all.

To Cressida Lindsay (young English poet and novelist), July 24, 1967:

Letters (*To an Imaginary Daughter*) aren't "written" like books. They are happenings when everything else including the typewriter is lost, and there's nothing to say except what always escapes and only later turns out to be the important thing. As always—not that huge goal we are all aiming at all the time (in our different ways, whatever it is)—but the milk bottle on somebody's doorstep we passed on the way. Always the incidental. Or rather, not "always" but, for us, on the hot line between different varieties of extinction (racial) when everyone knows (yes, even conductors and other silent travellers) that we are breathing just one breath at a time because the next one depends on whether the President's tranquilizer is working. Well—it's a long sentence, dangling, not by accident, but to communicate, dear Cressida, the dangling lives we all know we are living and just don't have the time to be articulate about because there are so many Important Things to Do—and it's in this 17,500-miles-a-second orbit we are swinging, that the in-betweens I am trying to catch now and then get down in the interstices—I call them not letters, not poems, but milk bottles.

Why milk bottles? Because Apollinaire discovered them in 1907 when he inaugurated the incidental in his poems, and the *avant garde* got going again making poems or paintings out of streets and garbage trucks and other milk bottles.

Why does it matter? Only because being alive matters—not for the huge geological mountains we think we are attaining, but for the bird feeder we watch to enjoy the titmouse sliding in for a mouthful.

Geology is the human enemy. Geology is Great Big Events, where even Ice Ages are infantile and you have to figure that it takes 30 million years to make the petrified forest of Mississippi. (I'm glad that state will go down, at least in geological history, not for its murders but for its beautiful stone trees.)

Yes, you can go on this way, typing out the little zeros while the Big Books wait to get done—provided you love each other as we do, we poor stupefied victims of writing disease. No wonder Shakespeare and Homer, etc. left it all for someone else to pick up and patch together and get into print. The fun was over after it had inadvertently slipped out onto the stage.

I hope you will not follow anything I say, because it will take you away from Good Sense and lead you to disaster, from which I can save you only at the very last moment when nothing else counts except that we were together once, circa 2,000 A.D.

The rest is not silence.

4

To an Imaginary Daughter

EDITOR'S INTRODUCTION

Trying to write an introduction for this chapter from To an Imaginary Daughter *is like trying to catch a sunbeam in a butterfly net.*

I could say: It's done in a casual style . . . but it's also formalized poetry. Or, it looks like prose on the page but it resounds like poetry in the mind.

I could say: Here we find Walter making epigrams. But what he makes is too open-ended, too freighted with meaning, too elliptical to be called epigrams. I could say: Here Walter clowns with us—he lies and he cheats, he postures and he postulates, he hides in evasions. Yet behind his clowning he is saying profound things.

Maybe I could try to make it simple and say: Here we

find Walter writing a long letter to an imaginary daughter who is away at college, and he is indulging himself in fatherly advice to the young. But it's a lot more than a letter to a co-ed, and to really appreciate it you need to bring to it some experience in the University of Hard Knocks and Lost Hopes. Besides, what he's advising is that you resist advice, make your own mistakes . . . and your own happiness.

About all I can say is: Here is Walter the Cosmic Ad Agency copywriter making advertisements for the more mysterious aspects of human existence.

–R. G.

To an Imaginary Daughter

In the beginning, it was really different, but nobody bothered to make a note of it. You know how careless we are about writing.

All we have is what's left after we forget.

In the other world, father really writes daughter. Here, it's just a make-believe, because it's today—and only yesterday is what we know. But if you wait long enough, the tape recorder begins to roll the other way, and you hear the return track sound as if it were going forward.

Of course, history is always being written afresh. Music, for instance. There is morning music, afternoon music, night music. In between there is also no music. That's the hardest to quote because nobody believes it. After all, it's not Mozart.

It's the same way with places. Somewhere else people are quite different. Only we never get there in time. By the time we arrive they have changed back into what we knew they were going to be before we left. Alice knew this when the Red Queen told her you have to travel twice as quick as you possibly can to get there.

It boils down to who shoots whom first.

—And from the hip. There's no time for anything else.

5:35 A.M.—A little break . . . And what better break than a note to my darling daughter who understands better than anyone the awful pause when the night music winds up at 5:30 and the day music doesn't start until 6 A.M.

These are the important things in the world that nobody ever mentions—the dead moments, the in-betweens.

That's the spot to celebrate the next geophysical year, with all instruments keyed to catch the invisible tune that some crazy underwater fish is releasing into the Gulf Stream.

When you get to the University of Chicago, will you kindly take up these matters with the authorities? Insist on the kind of courses that actually prepare you for the decisive moments when nothing happens and you are completely on your own, nowhere.

In spite of all this, believe me I understand the name on the doorbell. It means that you exist all by yourself—independently of the United Nations, IGY satellites and the baby you sit with.

Everybody thinks they want to be together. But you can't be together unless you are there, and that means that the postman can reach you.

Yes, the telephone books lie, the indices in the library lie, the registrars at the university don't know whether you are in Wisconsin or Michigan; only the mailman tells the truth; only the monkey on the organ grinder's string dances; only the whistle of the postbox opening and closing says to everybody: She is here—complete with teeth by Wolfman, psychoses by Pratz and heartbreak by etc.

How can we expect the boys to understand—they are so young? That, however, is not the problem. The sad thing is they refuse to grow up—ever. They never have their names on the mailbox even when they do. That's the dream world the music explodes. And of course they are tone-deaf like all the fishes in the brook.

I mention it so we shouldn't forget that whose name is on the mailbox counts a great deal. . . .

Only don't forget your handkerchief. You can never tell when the bleeding will start and the tears will run and the streets will stop and the traffic will go straight up without end, as it should, and it will be very quiet, thank God, for a change, and nobody wailing this and that and pass the salt, please, again and again and again.

Maybe now—just before it's too late I am getting the drift—the word is Catharsis. It doesn't make any difference what you say tomorrow—it's the top that blows off now that tells.

It's only what drives you more and more openly to suicide that saves your life—always just as the curtain is getting ready to drop.

If it can be said any other way, it's not a poem. Otherwise, I am that savage at your nerve ends you never believe. A loves X, A hates X—what's the difference is a sentence. Watch your sentences—no danglings! Everything to the period—the final dot that says it all!

I think the craziest words of all are "all is over," when everybody knows the next page is just beginning.

The idea behind the poem is to say nothing very circumspectly so nobody will suspect you have double-crossed him. The first rule: Never give the listener a break; always hint at unlimited reserves; be strongest at the end where it counts.

The issue is: Who exhausts whom first? Once the poet has the listener tight in his grasp, the poor auditor is helpless, believes anything he is told; even has the illusion he likes it.

Never be an amateur; be so slick everyone thinks you are improvising. And of course these are the elementary house rules—like not wetting the bed—said only to emphasize the obvious. Nothing else can be heard.

You will be forgiven everything but boredom. On that front, who can compete with the rocks?

It's more amusing not to be frantic. In the poem of it there is always time for one more drink, one more pose, one more kiss—always five minutes more for the love of it.

I've decided to start writing my final quartets. One problem is I can still hear a little. This I am trying to overcome by not listening to what I am saying—only to what the music says and to what the wild waves are saying and what you are saying—and others.

Only now, at 60, I begin to realize that all my life I have been stuck with hearing. I have had to learn how to be deaf. Then the music the wind puts into your head gets heard. You start floating with Blake and you stop flirting with posters.

5

Loving You in the Fallout

EDITOR'S INTRODUCTION

People who know them feel it had something to do with the shock Lillian suffered the night the FBI pulled the 2 A.M. raid on Walter and his typewriter, took him out of his home and tossed him in jail for having subversive thoughts. But it didn't happen that night—it happened later, after he got out of jail.

They were driving to Cleveland and Lillian was at the wheel. She pulled out to pass on a two-lane highway and before she could get by and back in line they almost crashed into an oncoming car. Maybe she had had all the shocks she could take in one lifetime; maybe part of her just refused to go along with it any more. Whatever the cause, whatever went into the making of it, she suffered a stroke and her left side has been paralyzed ever since.

During the summer of '65, she went to an experimental clinic in Hungary for one last attempt to regain movement in her left side. Loving You in the Fallout *is from letters Walter wrote her while she was there.*

–R. G.

Loving You in the Fallout

Some people pity the poor old couple living an offbeat life way out here in Mosquito Grove. Sensible people at our age move to the suburbs or Florida (as my brother used to urge) but why down here in outcast Five Acres in the backlands of the sand and pines—not just an hour from Philadelphia or two-and-a-half from New York but a Roman aqueduct away from the heart of things where judgments are really made and people live according to recognizable status?

If we came to our senses, we would find ourselves in a modern little apartment on a one-way street, with an elevator and bleached furniture and no muss, and with light and heat included in the $165 monthly, instead of our disreputable $24 payments on the mortgage.

It isn't as if we were proselytizing, trying to build a colony of independent thinkers or single taxers or another Brook Farm; or that our goals are country goals—gardens, terraces, hedges. Indeed, if this were a proper place, a ranch-level house with picture windows, well manicured, well sprinkled, the distance from downtown would vanish.

All we have done is to move one of our ill-kempt Paris flats out here to the woods. We are so proud that we moved the outhouse indoors and transformed the wood stove into an electric range. The open fireplace is now for fun, and an oil-burner keeps us basically warm. . . . All these modern improvements over 16 rue Denfert Rochereau, where we took showers in our portable canvas tub with a hose for cold water and a dipper for hot!

Out here in Weymouth, we are as far from the United States of our children as we were 30 years ago. Except that somehow the tables have been turned. In 1926, when I gave up butter for poetry, and New York for unheated flats in Florence and Paris, it was my elders who disapproved and thought we were crazy. And my father was not really surprised when my foreign ways in the 20's led me in the middle 30's to the Revolution. I had become tainted abroad. First, poetry; then communism.

Now we get no disapproval from the children for our fundamental relation to art and politics—it's just the surface manifestations of our off-color life in the nonconforming cottage in the former ocean bed that isn't even an artist's colony. The poem to justify the ways of God to man has been written. Our problem is to write a book to justify the ways of parents to children.

True, we have certain execrable habits. The keeping-papers habit is the worst; not just important papers, not just letters and carbons, but every scrap of paper that enters this house finds it much harder to get out than get in. We are surrounded by decades of magazines, newspapers, leaflets, pamphlets dating back to pre-World War II. We are living literally on top of our past lives. For quantities of papers, manuscripts, etc. have found their way into the cellar, where they keep the squirrels and mice happy and make splendid graves for the little ones that can't survive the doses of Zurd we have spread around.

Moving to the city would of course mean getting rid of the accumulated library middens of the past twenty years. Here I have no defense, except that it takes as much creative effort to destroy writing as to write it, and I just don't have the gusto I had when I made a fire of our old papers our last day in Paris, and even on the returning ship continued to discard papers that fluttered behind us like ghostly gulls most of the way across the Atlantic . . . to Mays Landing.

You say the day-long exercises are driving you crazy with

fatigue, you can't take any more of the lonesomeness and you make the whole experience sound more like torture than cure, and all the daughters except Mike say I should tell you to come home and I just wrote Mike:

I think Lillian's Budapest experience has been great for her and she will never be as unself-reliant again (as if there were so many decades ahead to prove that!). Anyway you look at it, when you are living, living is infinite, consists of all the possibilities of each instant, a continually exploding supernova of being here alive now. If it weren't we'd all have shot our brains out millennia ago. Who could stand dying all our lives? It's more fun to live. So Lillian takes out all her dying gripes—her King Learisms on us—gives the whole external mess the worst oaths she can swear, and I am reminded of the Divine who preached at the death of that beautiful young princess, "If you would know how great she was, think how terrible you feel that she's gone."

So she lives finger by finger, much closer to the real trapeze between complete rejection and possible survival than any of us know, except Dante in his more inspired passages in the Inferno.

I think maybe it's us little Two Eyes who are cock-eyed and take for granted our beautiful walks and breaths and bowels and sleeps and eats and two-handed typing. As my old friend Gurdieff used to say, most of us aren't conscious of being alive. We go round in little dreams of motion. That is impossible for Lillian. She cannot dream her life away. Each instant is an unceasing agony of surviving to the next agony, and there is no daylight ahead out of this rock cavern of the underworld of what it feels like to have to make a dead arm live.

How can we tell her what to do? There is a million-mile star space between the whole and the unwhole. It's that gap across being dead that nobody yet has crossed (Shakespeare reminds us). I tread here in this no man's land very softly, knowing only how little I know and how little the most loving of us can share what the dead arm knows and can't give the high sign about.

Yes, I know there is a world of the dead—the dead arms, the dead legs, the unmoving lips. And they know it, too. The great army of the thalidomide grownups who lack something.

Have you noticed how, when families are together, the children form a group of their own? There's a magnet between the young that draws them together, that world of play and the inexpressible things they know they have that the grownups don't share. The world of babble and jump and claw and knock-out and cry and laugh and jump. . . . All drawn together by what they know only they can do together—the hop-skip-and-jump world.

That's the world of the handicapped, too, that cannot help keeping all of us little Two Eyes outside. But let two of them get together even on the phone, like Maria, our neighbor, and Lillian—and the flow begins. They don't talk about the way they don't walk or move their left hands—it's just that the invisible fluid of being cast-outs in an alienated world brings them close in a no man's land nobody crosses who walks "normal" or two feet and feeds and washes normally with two hands.

So the arrogance I feel in any of us little Two Eyes telling one-armed Lillian what to do. Orpheus had to go to hell to bring back Eurydice. Can't we ever learn that?

Just because Lillian walks the surface of the earth in her special way, doesn't mean those little pitchforks aren't biting and burning and piercing her left side all the time. The hell of this is very simple—it just doesn't end. At best, there's a turn in the road somewhere ahead where you cast off a few pitchforks and live coals, but you still have to walk on the fire, and learn not to show it, to look and talk and chew the fat as in the other world.

It's easier to communicate with the nebula known as The Crab, from which we get radio noises that don't say a thing to us except that it's very hot, like three billion degrees, than to wigwag across the semaphore of being one-armed in a two-armed world. But if you look at it the other way, the handicapped are we who never can feel what they live; and to think we do and can tell them what to do is the real insanity, a parallel in our "peaceful way" of the marines thinking they can tell the Vietnamese via napalm and B-52 bombers how to live (as President Johnson says) "in peace."

But there is no peace in the world for the one-legs and one-arms. It's just lesser and greater degrees of torment and curses at why should it have been Me? What did I do? A million Jobs cursing God, but there is no God, so even your hemiplegic curses roll back on you with the thunder of the inevitable—the laws of chance that rule this world of statistics so that you for no reason at all have one ear instead of two and Marianthe has almost none.

I look around the streets and rooms for people who are minus something or are in wheel chairs or on crutches. When I see a man with a seeing-eye dog—my heart jumps and I cry "Comrade!" only softly, so as not to embarrass him.

And this other world of us—what are we doing with it that makes us so proud? I could understand telling Lillian what she should do about staying until the end of her therapy, or getting out to stop the misery now, if we were living in a Garden of Eden with no sound but dropping apples and lovers kissing. But in this horror of Mississippi in Los Angeles and burning infants alive in Vietnam, where do we come off telling her to rejoin this horror instead of surviving as best she can and getting whatever she can from that other hell of the cerebral palsy and polios and strokes? At least, somewhere they were innocent. While over here, as Len Chandler says in his poem, "there are no innocent." All we can do at best is share the guilt and not tell others how to rule their lives.

I hear the Aztec scream your clenched teeth
    can't utter and I see the serpent nightmare
    burn up the throwing away crutches your hemi-

plegia whispers *I want to be.* And I'm whispering back:
In the Pyramids where no is yes
I won't love you
because I love you
on a rock
ants don't get into
because there is
no rock I love you
can't whisper away.

So this is it—our youth, our age—for love and poetry, all ages are the same—56, 66, 90, or 20. And that, I think, is the big discovery of the Space Age: We don't die anymore as we did. We live each instant as if it were the last, at the edge of somebody's nuclear button. Of course, that isn't the poem, and we all feel and write about the usual things—spring, love, children and, just now, a red cardinal hopping across the grass looking for edibles, completely unaware of the strontium 90 count.

Does that explain why all our books tend toward the same title—$E = MC^2$? It's just the universal dateline, reporting the 11th Commandment: Thou Shalt Not Overkill!

Driving down 9W, and other paths parallelling the Hudson from Newburgh and Peekskill and Nyack, past Haverstraw and Letchworth Village and Nanuet and Spring Valley and New City, and all those other signs of cities and towns where we left so much behind so many years ago (including Angela's birth in another one of those road signs), I thought, if you live long enough, as we are doing, you don't die blow by blow like somebody hammering you on the head so the hairs get gray and disappear etc.—no, not that kind of murder—we belong to the onion family, and peel off layer after layer until we get to the last remembrance of pure bone—and everybody says (3,000 A.D.) "my God! another pithecanthropus erectus you could never mistake for an eel, which sheds its skin too but has no head to remember where skin after skin was shed, and so died."

It would be good, perhaps, now that we are finally moving for the last time, to go to some utterly new place—like Alaska or Peru—but those will only be places to visit, because blood is thicker than distance and now there is this last move from Mays Landing to Peekskill on the Hudson, where we started out in the pre-children age driving up to the Catskills or among reservoirs to see the Indian country on week-ends in the 20's. (Well, that sentence got lost somewhere.) Anyhow, now we're getting to the last layers of the onion of remembrance—and at least we never before have passed by that particular Washington Lane or Boulder Drive to which we are moving so we can peel off what's left near children and friends and spare them the awful job of digging us out of Five Acres.

Yes, we had been burying ourselves in the little house we found so unexpectedly (following that ad—"a hideaway") 13 years ago, when all we were looking for was a cabin we would own for week-ends instead of having always to drive and drive to get away from Philly.

So we found Yucatan on the Upper Atlantic—the sand barrens the ocean left behind just a few millennia ago—where nothing grows except ants and gnats and wasps and birds, unless you work the soil with love and care, which of course I never did (and you couldn't do the last seven years), so I doubt whether anyone will ever know we passed this way, except perhaps for the cesspool we had dug. So mankind comes and goes and leaves its scats behind.

It's amazing how sentimental you can get about a desert spot where all we did was love and make poems and work. Our roots here are very thin—except for Maria and a few in Mizpah—our passing will make no dent and there'll be no farewell parties. And yet, much was done here before the onion gave out.

Ah yes—I just remembered—the chickadees and titmice will miss us and wonder where the bird feeders went to—I mean, not us, but the wooden bird feeders we kept full for them. Hoyle, the astronomer, says birds are the end of the line of that particular animal development—and they never will have bigger brains and be able to love us as we love them.

So, back we go where we started from when we returned from Paris in 1935. And yet, not exactly—I mean not to the same Rockland County Road with Fraenkel, our old friend, across the way, and a Fair for Loyalist Spain at the big estate toward Haverstraw, given by a sympathizer to help raise money for milk for Spanish children.

But it's the up-and-down hills of glacier land, with forests and views to which we return like trawlers from the new Yucatan of North America where only Chichen Itza is missing. We get so used to sand lots and dreary level stretches of pre-jungle, that we begin to love our desolate Weymouth on the Sand Barrens—not for any scenic reason—but just because we lived there together with it; so many years we did so many things.

Who else ever got a kick driving to Somers Point or to Vineland? Or returning from Bratislava or Moscow to our sand road with its tree roots protruding more and more, so even the postman said we'd better chop them off before we break a tire.

What we leave behind is the routine of postboxes and Mullica Rivers we are fond of just because we visited them when day's work was done, instead of some nearby Grand Canyon which would have been a homesite for us if we lived on the other side of Gallup, New Mexico.

So it's really good-bye—not to the ocean but to the ocean bed we have lived on for 13 years and when we leave, it will flow back over all our memories of the fish we ate on the beach or fed to the gulls.

About the home we are buying, the owner said, all he wanted was the privilege some day to drive back and look at it once again. But that's a present dream that vanishes as his new house becomes home. Who cares that we once lived on Regent St.? Or Kingsessing? Or Chancellor? Or rue Denfert

Rochereau? All those layers of places have peeled off us with hardly a trace, except in our hair which is the last place to go. I mean, when all your hair goes and even the memory of hair is lost, then you are really gone for good.

What's left now is just us, loving here or there or anywhere, because home is always where Walter and Lillian are together.

All our valises are packed, as they were just before Athens blew up in a blaze of poetry and sculpture. Any letter that doesn't suggest that is a disgrace to the amoeba in us. Poetry isn't a way out. It just points up the fact that it's the little details that count—like whether we finish with vine leaves in our hair or gamma buttons.

It isn't just the imminence of nuclear explosions that is fissioning us into unstable isotopes. There is a pulverization of ourselves going on during peace. In fact, that's what peace has become in the United States: molecular orbits of our multi-selves, swirling around ground zero ahead of time.

If you don't know this sensation, even in Budapest, you're not a good *Americano del Norte*; you're living in a rosebowl of nonexistent homogeneity.

I'm not trying to settle anything with this gabble—just getting if off my chest. In tomorrow's glass museum of man —no heroes, just the earth in an extrapolation of human tissue. We are swinging to peace across the perpendicular trapeze of the Great Divide. And none of us will ever be the same.

Whose inter-galactic footprints are we following?
    Have we lost our sense of galaxies?
Can't we master the quiet sun
    of not saying too much
before our language fades with Eric the Red's
    among the cosmic clichés of outer space?

Dear Fellow-Tree: If I don't tell you how will you know it's the summer of the mimosa? It took 13 years to arrive, starting when you stuck a little nothing sprig in the ground in front of our cottage the year we took over these five acres of sand in the pine barrens. The ocean only got out of here and retreated 25 miles to Ocean City about 20,000 years ago. And looking at the green zero that has grown so slowly without bearing a single rosy bud, it seemed as if the soil were undecided which way the weather is heading and might be preparing to go under water for another Sea Age.

All around South Jersey, every summer, we would drive and you would point out elsewhere the shivering, pinkish mimosa erupting like a fancy French dessert. But our mimosa was a stunted boy-girl, sexless, without a hair on its naked green body. Each year it grew taller and taller and never grew out of the green stage. It seemed our acres were doomed—and we talked about why a new mimosa should sprout flowers anyhow on this forthcoming ocean bed of ours. For we know that the future here belongs not to us but to the immortal sea and when the Greenland ice cap starts to melt a little faster, as it will from time to time, and the summers last a little longer, as they will, the water level along our beautiful, green Atlantic shore will rise that fatal two inches that starts the reciprocal weather action the other way, toward the sea bottoms where New York and Weymouth and other pleasant landscapes are destined to disappear below the tides.

But this summer for the first time our mimosa has taken the fateful turn away from death by sea and entered its blossoming pink life. Everybody's talking about war and privilege and there's no room to spend a second on that vast future our flowering mimosa has finally decided to enter. And believe me, for no reason except that it just happens to be the way the earth finally decided to keep moving ahead another galactic second, the year of the mimosa.

I would call it a suspension of life—a pip of mort hung in an oil emulsion. You look through the glass bottle at the bubble—and that's me—apparently alive—a glob of glub glub continually drowning in the absence of you.

You take a car, for instance—what good is all this airconditioned coolth if it doesn't warm you? Or the clean house without you to praise ultra-cleanliness—or the neighbor from Mizpah, Mister Davis, whom I made it my business to find this week, and who is en route this moment to cut our grass and clean up the grounds—or the spick-and-span-cellar—spicked by Jeanie—everything, books, papers, etc., *et al*, in boxes.

So it goes—nature abhors a vacuum—and I'm the bubble in the vacuum. What fun is it to open mail alone? What good is it to watch birds at the feeder? I haven't even filled them again with the new bag of birdseed. The birds don't know I love them, and if you don't love them too, it's just a humanitarian effort to fill the feeders—or would you call it an ornithological effort?

It's no use even being nostalgic at leaving this dumpyard of last year's leaves and broken benches—I can't be sorry alone. I just go from hour to hour working, sleeping, and, in between, a galactic sadness at the swift passing of human footsteps. I'm living in terms of thousand-year intervals. I drive up the Expressway to Philadelphia and cross the Walt Whitman Bridge and all I see are the runis of 3,000 A.D. that we have left behind. I'm supposed to be the glad eye, the ever young, the big heart, etc., etc., but all I see from my lonesome bubble is ten centuries ahead—long past water shortages, air pollution and all human damages, and I can't imagine what the babies of 2,000 A.D. will be crying for. Certainly not the smog of what we might have been that we left for them to play over.

So—without you, my bubble of eternity just goes swoosh swoosh—a big oily tear is all I am without you. And all I can send you is a tiny air hole of a kiss.

Absently.

I have been reading Gordon Childe, the archeologist, who says only two things last—poetry and pottery. Now Bertrand

Russell calculates the mathematical possibility of erasing whole areas of the earth in five minutes of "nuclear exchange."

What happens then to the lasting qualities of pottery or poetry? I don't mean in the unknown future, but today, as I write you on the hot line between hope and disaster?

How long can this go on—trying to count-down the delicious word that says it all before the typewriter explodes?

What other age ever fired their pottery and poems from such launching pads?

Well, as I told you when you were here, don't call it "poetry"—call it "paper-pottery." Because in the Great Explosion, if it comes, nobody will know the difference. And if it doesn't come, all our cliff-hanging eternities will seem as old-fashioned as elegies by a dinosaur.

Living, too, had become an art in your half of the 20th century. One has to wash one's hands with carbolic acid every hour to keep clean in this hospital of the United States and the result is to burn yourself to the bone.

But at least one burns.

—Which is one step ahead of a stubbed match.

Will this kill you? The life that counts is the narrowest escape. Otherwise we don't qualify for the final heat.

A good beginning: Get yourself a map of El Mundo, with Africa in the center, not the United States.

P.S. I once started writing a book of philosophy about all this. After 35 years I have two sentences left: (1) John Brown doesn't live by speeches, but by hanging; (2) the Kingdom of Heaven isn't within me; it's within you.

Yes, there are two classes in the world—angels and devils. My advice: master the old devil universe. Only that way can you get to the next futility. Then you are living! With the angels, of course.

In heaven one speaks to all the angels all the time and they have sense enough to be totally absorbed in nothing but what you're saying and never answer back. Down here, you can learn from them how to work that rarely used organ, the ear. (That way, *you* become the angel.)

> The act of you in my mind is sculptural.
> Coiling through the mould of my brain
> the thought of you cools into marble
> a monument of you as you have lain
> before me in the dark: I know the feel
> your fibres of fluid stone distill:
> Through my fingers pours the carnal skein
> of you: O love, I touch you. Not these hands:
>
> the phantom fingers of my being prove
> the mastery of structure in each vein,
> and chisel into light your body's true
> plasticity. In spaces where light bends
> through silent ethers of pure sense, O love,
> I reach, incalculably carved, You.

Is this the time to talk about poems? I know it seems crazy, but sometimes in the Age of Confrontation, anything else seems crazier. (Like today—reading Secretary McNamara's latest estimate—over a hundred million casualties on each side, the first five minutes of nuclear exchange.)

We are in danger of leaving here suddenly without ever knowing what it was like to be here in the first place. Art shows us not only what living felt like but what it could be.

That's what human history amounts to—a record that we mounted above the rocks, made something infinitely fragile that any mountain upthrust or H-bomb interval destroys without a quiver and yet, without it, the Whole Story remains a lava of nonsense that floods the cracks of the universe with cosmic glue.

The days used to ripple by like the Little Egg Harbor River along Sweetwater Road. Now you are gone, each day is a huge iceberg barely able to split off from time's arctic freeze. How long can this go on before our separated continent breaks up and we begin floating toward each other?

Yes, darling, all I'm trying
  to program on this typewriter
    is : *what are we?*
hoping to convince the next paleontologist
  who asks: *were they homo sapiens?*
not to count only our megatons of yesterday
  and miss the infinite calculus
  of trying to be lovers
today.

Love letters at 68 are not love letters at 40 or 20. Now you appreciate the important things, like not being in the hospital. It seems to me our lives are haunted by these kill-cure places. I keep thinking of my mother's hospital days on different floors, graded according to her ability to function. If she could only get to Floor 3, where you ate from plates and your door wasn't locked and people didn't beat each other and howl.

So–get well and keep us well. Our problem is to concentrate on the world's despairs, not our own–that is the only hope and the only cure.

In some other country, with a paralyzed left arm and leg, you might be handicapped; in this land of ours, where the national disease has become an invisible atrophy, anyone with half a brain left is that much ahead of the Chiefs of Staff. This is not a criticism–just a corrective, to get your orbit into its true coordinates. The game is to keep one archeological layer ahead of the human ice age that surrounds us.

There is a white Africa in the United States handicapped all the way to the bone cells. You should be proud of the tremendous responses you have kept alive in your one good arm and leg in this valley of the sea spores. Kindly answer this by return police dogs, and the only thing that counts any more–total disaster or triumph.

Yes, darling, if I talk now and then about outer space, maybe it's because I have returned here skeptical about the land future of our order of placentals. I can't help it—in fact, I fight against it—but science and something antenna-like inside my vertebrae assure me that the human race will never make it as is. We will do it better, as they are doing it better, Moscow, Budapest, *et al.* And more people will have better lives, in bigger cities, with less pollution, but I'm obsessed with the future where they will be a completely different set of air breathers and not even an old shoe left of you and me and all our billions who did it so sweetly in the Magellan Age.

Anyhow, it's reassuring to have a framework in which to exercise our hands and typewriters. It leaves one really nothing to worry about except to make the present as bearable as can be and get to the next stage as quickly and painlessly as possible. And, of course, get rid of the pterodactyl monsters among us as rapidly as can be.

Just a note to let you know everything down here is bleeding.

The piano is leaking, the sun is asleep. We have caught fire. It's one of those mines that has to be sealed.

Our conflagration is so far below surface, it can't be reached by radar.

But in the carboniferous depths where our love affair begins, the final curtain is just going up.

My problem is I just take it for granted the pueblos will last much longer than the Pentagon. Is this unpatriotic?

Please reply by return laser. But bounce it back from Andromeda to make sure we know where we are. You have a disease too. You take me seriously. When all I'm trying to do is to imitate the laugh somebody is smiling on the other side of the Crab.

I mean, it's the Heisenberg theory up-to-date—if you don't know how funny you are you don't know how to get there. I want a computer that will instantaneously translate all the 148 southwestern languages into their original poems.

i.e., by our arrow heads we shall be known.

The other night I dreamed I bent down low over this dried-up old ocean bottom and took big mouthfuls of sand and tried to learn the sand language. Oh I know as I spit out the sand all I heard was splutter splutter splutter. And that was the song.

We are a restless generation—the new Bedouins without camels—and we all have this in common, that none of us have been long where we are. Maybe that's one reason we all feel a common humanity, our morality is on the move, never gets used to one cemetery. Naturally we approach the new cremation—not like the Etruscans who kept their ashes (those who had the dough) in sculptured alabaster urns—but like the *Americanos del Norte* who throw their flames anywhere knowing it's just a matter of time when they'll be moving again anyway.

Thus one great triumph emerges: We have advanced from the Brooklyn Cemetery Days. You can still see those as you drive out from Manhattan to Long Island—vast stretches of the dead buried in inaccessible plots where fewer and fewer of us go to visit our forefathers. We are too busy moving to bother about the immovable. Poor old things—why didn't they move while they still had the time?

In my father's day his generation still celebrated "*jahrzeit*" —the anniversary of his father's or mother's death when the family cemetery plot would be visited by us with flowers and a silent prayer. "Honor thy father and thy mother. . . ." We have changed all that hangover from the Greeks. I just feel an awful repulsion driving past those vacant lots in Brooklyn where everybody's forefathers occupy the ghettos of the dead. What a crime when the living are piled ten high in a room in Bedford-Stuyvesant!

I don't see how anybody can be wistful about "the old days." People lived in one spot all their lives and then got buried next door. Immobility. We have become our own microwaves, feel much closer to Andromeda and other civilizations on the other side of Cygna XI than to our great grandfathers. We are tied to the next house and the next, not that horrible dungeon of the immobile past.

So we are going through this common operation we have known many times, cutting out this particular umbilical cord of Five Acres for another house. And it's a scientific fact that no matter how buggy the air, nor how full the sand is of crab grass and midges and bugs, and how near we still are here to the ocean bottoms, any place where you have lived needs a surgical operation to get rid of. So we are saying good-bye to this cancer of our past in Weymouth, New Jersey, to join the great migration of never dying in the same place twice.

My disease is to appear sane. At 67 I am aware that this fixation is incurable. Nor is there any use mentioning it. Nobody believes me except you, and you have grown so used to it, it's like living in the same cage with a grizzly bear. You also are a little grizzly bear, you think.

You see how communicable my disease it?

If I say to the Doctor—Doctor, my blood pressure is under control, but I know I am not right.

What are the symptoms? he asks.

So I leave without a pill.

Believe me, darling, this is serious.

Because if you can't locate where you are, how can you define who you want to be?

It's the final identity that counts. The answer is neither one thing nor the other. Who thinks he's all sane? I'm just revealing the other side of the world mirror where we are caught between murder in Vietnam, mayhem in Mississippi and tomorrow's Flying Wallendas.

What I am talking about is geology. How do we stack up against the rocks? Is our love a geological spore incidental to the mountain building of the earth's crust?

I'm saying it's more complicated than ice. I can give you only a hint of the direction from which the wind is blowing and where the fish always bite, expecting nothing from you (although you will supply it all).

For Lillian, Gardening

The warm heart scratch
    of our being here together
doesn't kid the azaleas.
    Over Indian Ocean
snow gathers
    clouds from Aladdin's lamp
skids through
    time's blizzards
to light
    our victory
in ice.
    And still
this footprint of our love
    cries *you you you*
        to the end,
one human instant
    worth all
earth's senseless eternities.

It just struck me, darling, that I'm living under an illusion that come Thanksgiving when you will be back, with you and me tucked away in the other Five Acres at Boulder Drive, Peekskill, things will quiet down and there won't be this one-step-forward, two-steps-backward dance of new things piling up each day to do, with some leftovers from the day before and the day before that, and so on back to Father Amoeba who started it all looking in his rear mirror for the primeval swamp and instead finding eternal us—no no it won't get simpler. This is the new pace, constantly accelerating at the Newton rate twice the square of the approach, always more, always more complicated, and always time to say I love you which is what all the fuss is about anyway—I mean, otherwise where would the little babies come from in the first place and you know how I always said—everybody loves their own baby more than anybody else's (and God said it a few years ago—telling Moses let them go out and multiply). And now, with the deadline past for getting married status and deferment from Vietnam, that tremendous rush at the marriage bureaus so that the marriage agents put them thru the ringer at three minutes per couple to help them beat the Johnson deadline (and some Russian agent said, looking at the mob of young newly marrieds, "Good God, don't tell me they'd rather pfuck than Pfight!")

Well—to get back—I must destroy that illusion of fewer complications. It will always be another multiple of another factor of another poem of being alive.

And this will not get less involved. Don't let's have that illusion. We are living thru the dying days of a dragon who is mortally wounded but still lashing its tail and snorting napalm and juggling H-bombs on its horned snout. So how can it get simpler? Always one degree higher, Eluard said. And Lenin too—organization, organization, organization. . . .

and love

equals

you me

Driving home(!) from Camden after the signing of the "closing" papers for sale of the house, leaving the Delaware River behind, zooming along the pine barrens, haunted by geology. These roadways in and out of Philadelphia and its Devonian epoch whose ocean comings and goings we have known for 29 years (since we moved to Atlantic City from New City, 1938) are engrained in us the way fossil footsteps of dinosaurs and other fishy spines are chiseled in the rock caverns. When we disappear from this scene, its geology goes along with us. Now I am trying to study up on the glacier movements of the Hudson Valley to know what ice age we are heading for. The earth is going to be different for us, so how can we be the same at Boulder Drive off Mountain Road back of a long history of mountain folding and vast stony upheavals of the Appalachians and Adirondacks and Catskills? We are receding from the ocean bottoms. This is good-bye to the Yucatan of the North. We shall never find the island of the flamingos in the land of the Algonquins. We can see now that we visited Chitzenitza just in time, before it disappeared in our stone-age past when we were ocean creatures scouting the Mullica Rivers and Oyster Creeks of our recent youth. I don't think there's a surface of the earth that doesn't haunt some race or family, and it can be the barest tundra or the pueblos of Mesa Verde or the Zuni and Hopi lands of the Grand Canyon. I mean that landscape we carry with us doesn't have to be pretty; it just has to have been lived and there it stays—and we think (without saying a word) about those quickly growing ferns that sprout after a forest fire has leveled the ground and not only cover the ashlike trees but have the veins of their leaves imprinted in our bones. This is the past we can't ever get rid of—the landscape, the earth we lived thru when Angela was four and the twins were 14 and other landmarks of our restless epoch as we moved from house to house.

I never felt this geological drift when we shifted from Paris to Tunis to Florence and Berlin and France and Brooklyn Heights and Union Heights and all our other migrations. Passing those old territories later, I never felt we were part of them or they of us, but now, this last imprint of the pine barrens and the Schuylkill Expressway and the flowering mimosas are not left behind. We are hardening and it is they who harden with us. Now we carry our poor sand barrens and scrub oak inside us wherever we go. We are not only the people with whom we lived, we are encrusted with inanimate things, and not only inanimate. How can we ever see a chickadee or a nuthatch hanging upside down on his claws pecking away at a bark without that Five-Acre birdary we grew inside of us stirring and wondering, is he the same nuthatch?

I hate all this to be invisible. I wish there were holidays when our fossil insides would be turned inside out and we could parade our old geologies. But maybe I'm making it all up, and in a month or six months it'll all be so far down the bloodstream we will never look at each other when we see a spruce or a swamp magnolia and say nothing, knowing our fossil insides have given each other the high sign: "Ah yes, we were there!"

Anyhow, the climate is changing. The whole Eastern Seaboard is drying out, the water is being wrung from it and soon there won't be anymore to drink and we will all have to move upstream to Canada or Baffins Bay or Greenland. I have absolutely no faith in the permanent earth. I see it crumbling to dust before our own eyes and soon all that will be left is the invisible portrait, its final claws left in the human beings who could not survive there and carried the landscape away even before it disappeared forever. We are on the threshold of one more Aleutian Drive. Our future is moving with the Eskimo dogs and the ice floes of other places other times. The only death is to stay behind.

Just struck me that when you returned from Cleveland to Philadelphia, seven years ago, and were taken from the plane to the Episcopal Hospital, and stuck in a bed there until plans could be made for you, I felt worse than I had any time in the months since you had the stroke. Now the trip was over. We were back in home territory. We could no longer see ourselves as travelers, with you sick in a strange town. Now we had to be on our own. And I realized that whatever there was left of you, there was nobody else who would ever love me as you do. A selfish thought; I acknowledged that to myself, thinking of me, not you and your calamity and what you would miss without your left arm and leg. So—there is this selfishness—or self-concern in love, at any rate between grown-ups. I suppose parents don't have that feeling about children. Maybe they love them in a pure way. But between us, who would love us as we do?

If this seems awkward, out of place, not in keeping; just think of others. Who loved Robert Browning the way

Elizabeth did? She couldn't even count the ways. That is the tragedy of Shakespeare's sonnets—not that he had loved and lost, but that he would never be loved that way again. So—no doing away with the I factor. And this makes the mystery of Whitman's love life one that continues to baffle us. "Call me the tenderest lover," he said. And we have evidence in the letters he got from soldiers that literally hundreds of men loved him "as a father, a mother." The mystery is how he, the great lover, got along as he did for 73 years without one permanent love *from* someone.

"Who will ever love you as I did?" the girl cries out on the road to her lover in the last scenes of *La Dolce Vita.* Maybe men are just incapable of that kind of love, even when they think they are? Maybe we are better killers than lovers? I have no doubt, as you know, that our small role as fertilizers will be taken care of otherwise after the next Ice Age. This way is too complicated. Women only have to learn that they don't really need us. And that, by the way, may explain a cry I have been unable to locate in my work. And yet I feel sure it exists somewhere on some page. A woman crying out: "I don't need you; I can live without you! I DON'T NEED YOU!" This goes on echoing, the truly final word—the ultimate triumph, the ultimate tragedy and only death—to be able to live alone. Who wants it? Besides, it's an illusion, a hangover from the dog-eat-dog days of human pre-history.

So, as I started to say, I need you because nobody will ever love me that way. And even at 68 ½ you cannot live without:

Splitting the bread
    Dividing the sun
Kissing each other's cheeks
Putting ribbons on the storms
    Turning each body into a flower
        And time and space
make the padlocks sing. . . .

At the last moment in Five Acres I begin to understand ground rent. If the reference mystifies you, check it in the final pages of the final volume of Marx's *Capital*, or the letters he and Engels exchanged about this fundamental question in commodity relations.

Naturally, our ground rent is different (again that spiral difference which Marx would understand).

This is the toughest moving I have had since we dug out of the spiral underground of Paris, 1934, and we sat up with Henry in front of the fireplace at rue Val de Grace and burned up old papers, or gave what he wanted to him. (He began his notebooks, he wrote later, with that stuff we discarded.)

There the ground rent was paper and a few clothes and pictures. Not too much for us to load into a trunk or two and the few grips we loaded with the Fords and into our compartment in the train that took us to the *SS Gerolstein* and New York after a ten-year absence (plus twins and Mike).

Here, it's a 27-year rooting in the Delaware Valley, since we first arrived in Atlantic City, 1938, and then in Philly. At my age the roots are harder to dig up, not so pliable as in Paris, 1934. The back of the packing is broken, Nan said, pointing to the 120 boxes of books and clothes and linens. Now the main job is to excavate the lungs and heart.

And to think how innocently and light-weightedly this all started with a carry-all when I left New York, March 1926, and you added your grip when we got married in Paris, later that year.

How easily we shifted from apartment to apartment in Paris and then to Florence, and to North Africa, and back to Paris (Thuringen in between). We have gotten much too heavy. The ground rent should have been in reverse—I could have moved tons so easily in 1926 or 36 or even 46 when there were only pounds to budge—and now, the law of gravity operates and we get heavier with things as we grow older and find it very hard to lift up what we have and shift one more degree upward.

The interminable and unalterable law of ground rent: The

less strength I have to tackle the moving the more ground rent there is to move. I seem to be cemented to the earth —i.e., I am priceless in my old-age rent and don't have the strength any more to leave papers behind. It's just an insoluble equation—to weigh more and to be able to lift less. How are we ever going to get the rest of our weight out of this place by the deadline of October 1? Maybe we won't? Maybe some of us will be buried here, under the mimosa that only sprouts three flowers a year, or near the one holly that survives from all we planted? And I have a wonderful epitaph for the remains: Here lies a ton of bricks Walter and Lillian couldn't lift onto the last truck, left here as perpetual ground rent on the life that can't be moved.

I have written you how shallow our roots are here—and yet, there's something else that takes the place of the people around here we don't really know. We will never be able to live anywhere as long as we did in Paris, where the concierge, Madame Bigault, really belonged, and went every month to visit the graves of her grandparents in Montparnasse, only a few blocks away.

We won't live long enough in Peekskill to replace Larry who took me to his grandmother's last week, in Mizpah, to get some extra newspapers. "I know my way around," he told me as he opened the door of their little home and loaded the papers in our car.

"How long have they lived here?" I asked as we drove away. "Well, I'm not sure, but let me put it this way. My grandfather built that house—and that one (he pointed to the house we were passing next door)—that's the house he was born in."

You get the point? Ground rent in your own area, your own neighborhood, where you are rooted as the people around here are. That is what we will not replace. Not that we lived for the last 15 years among people who did have ground rent and weren't orbits circling all over the western globe as we have been the past 45 years.

We are now bankrupt, unable to store up enough relations

in the new city ever to know people who live where they have lived for generations. That's what the truck that takes us will leave behind—the ground rent that can't and won't be moved.

We are continual travelers in a shiftless world where no two generations sleep in the same ground and the rent for being here is never really paid.

And thus we cheat the universe, which is, I suppose, the responsibility of being human and never caught in the same crime in the same place twice.

Who was the Egyptologist
    said all history
        is just an hour old?
Of course! My darling infant love,
    our affair is just beginning
        on top of this newborn earth.
Our tiny fifty or sixty years
    slow down its spin around the dance floor
        about the weight of your pony tail
the North Star probably estimates at
    the braking power of a slice of grass.

We are such stuff as bric-a-brac is made of. And soon our little lives will be rounded by a moving van. We'll need a flotilla of them to get us out of here with all the tons of odds and ends of 40 years of housekeeping, book-hoarding and filing all pieces of paper, including *Paris Soir* 1934: BAGARRES ET EMEUTES—riots and fights—the names we almost gave the twins because they were born in those February days when we too were out in the streets demonstrating to save the Third Republic.

And when we arrive at Boulder Drive with all our belongings and the new helpers help us to unpack what the old helpers loaded, everybody will take it for granted those are things we left with. But you and I will know that they are not at all the same packages nor the same little boy and girl. We will have aged one billion years, and that is the final age.

I'm disgruntled with myself at my little melancholies in leaving this insect-breeding love-nest. I began the other day to sound like Tchaikovsky! Now I begin to feel Webern and Ives. We, the Concord conquerors, are moving to new victories, and, in the words of Eugene Debs, joy cometh in the morning.

Cows can be homesick. Pigeons can mourn over lost perches. We have time only for the next house, the next life, the next poem. That, I suppose, was what I had in mind yesterday when I said perhaps we should attach a little U-Haul trailer on the car and take with us the current work files, typewriter, paper, carbon, *et al.* En route Boulder Drive we might find an amusing place to spend a day or a year or a decade—a waterfall overlooking on one side, the Hudson River, on the other, Lake Como—and in the distance, Banff and the Canadian Rockies. I mean, you said you always wanted to live right on the water so we should be instantly ready to unpack the moment we see that pinnacle overlooking all the oceans, all the lakes, not excluding the Bay of Fundy. For me it's not the view of the water as much as those vast tides of the Bay of Fundy I always wanted to see. And, with our trailer behind us, why not? I can always sock out a page or two amidst the roaring surges of the Arctic seas. Maybe we should swap the car for one of those combination auto-boats so that when the tide rises we can float on?

I see endless voyages ahead. I announce triumph of eternal motion. We will defeat the roads and the wars and all the horrors of the past. We have nothing to lose but our age. And that is leaving us rapidly on two vans in the morning.

Your last Lochinvar youth WALTER